Pioneer Children of Appalachia

by Joan Anderson

Photographs by George Ancona

CLARION BOOKS
NEW YORK

To my father, who taught me his survival skills   –J.A.

To Maxine B. Rosenberg   –G.A.

Clarion Books
a Houghton Mifflin Company imprint
215 Park Avenue South, New York, NY 10003
Text copyright © 1986 by Joan Anderson
Photographs copyright © 1986 by George Ancona
All rights reserved.
For information about permission to reproduce
selections from this book, write to Permissions,
Houghton Mifflin Company, 2 Park Street, Boston, MA 02108
Printed in the USA

Library of Congress Cataloging-in-Publication Data
Anderson, Joan. Pioneer children of Appalachia.
Summary: Text and photographs from a living history
village in West Virginia re-create the pioneer life of
young people in Appalachia in the early nineteenth
century.
1. Pioneer children—West Virginia—Juvenile
literature. 2. Pioneer children—Appalachian Region,
Southern—Juvenile literature. 3. West Virginia—
Social life and customs—Juvenile literature.
4. Appalachian Region, Southern—Social life and
customs—Juvenile literature. 5. Frontier and pioneer
life—West Virginia—Juvenile literature. 6. Frontier
and pioneer life—Appalachian Region, Southern—Juvenile
literature. [1. Frontier and pioneer life—Appalachian
Region. 2. Appalachian Region—Social life and customs.
3. West Virginia—Social life and customs] I. Ancona,
George, ill. II. Title.
F241.A58   1986   975.4′57   86-2624
ISBN 0-89919-440-0

HOR 10 9 8 7 6 5 4

Introduction

Between 1790 and 1830, hundreds of Americans moved into the rugged hills and narrow hollows, or hollers, of what became the state of West Virginia. In those days long before supermarkets, factories, and cars, a pioneer family made almost everything it needed to survive. Children worked as hard as their parents and grandparents did.

This book re-creates the life-style of the fictional Davis family. The scenes were photographed at Fort New Salem in Salem, West Virginia, a living history museum celebrating the folkways of Appalachia. The museum, which is part of nearby Salem College, carefully preserves and teaches the traditional survival crafts of the pioneers.

*T*oday was special for Elizabeth Davis. Pa was taking her and Isaac to help Grandpa and Grandma over in the next holler. They would even stay the night.

Elizabeth almost never got to travel away from home. In pioneer families, girls and women remained close to the cabin. Boys and their fathers went off to do exciting things—hunt for meat, fell mighty trees, or help kinfolk and neighbors to build houses and sheds.

This year, though, Grandpa had more basket orders than usual. So before winter set in, Elizabeth and Isaac were going to help him.

Pa, his flintlock in the crook of his arm, hoped to spot a deer or even a rabbit. Everyone knew that a man worth his salt never arrived for a meal empty-handed.

As they strode along, the family sang "Froggie Went A-Courtin'" to set the pace. They still had to wade across Indian Run Creek and hike along Raccoon Run before they were within sight of Grandpa's place.

Elizabeth wondered if Ma was thinking about them now, back in the little cabin at Crooked Run.

Elizabeth remembered the lonely look on Ma's face as they said good-bye. Ma was expecting a baby, and everyone hoped it would arrive before the cold weather did.

Aunt Jane had come to the Davis cabin to help take care of things. Even so, Elizabeth and Isaac had done chores before starting out. Isaac helped Pa sharpen the axes to chop down trees at Grandpa's.

Elizabeth milked Bossie and fed the chickens. Next she gathered ashes from the hearth to fill the wooden hopper used for soapmaking. Then she placed a bucket under the hopper's spout to catch the water she poured through.

After Elizabeth had soaked the ashes and let the water drip through ten or more times, the bucket was full of lye water. This strong solution was mixed with fat to make soap.

While Elizabeth was away, Ma and Aunt Jane would finish the job. They would boil the lye in a big kettle with beef tallow. The smell was always horrible! Elizabeth was glad she could leave before that part of the process.

Ma and Aunt Jane would stir the mixture until it thickened. Then they would pour it into gourds and old dishes, leaving it to semi-harden. Afterward, they would cut it into cakes and leave them to harden in the sun.

There sure would be plenty of soap
for the laundry days ahead, Elizabeth
thought.

Just after the Davises crossed Indian Run Creek, Isaac spotted something.

"Hey, Pa, look over there," he whispered. "A rabbit—good size, too."

Pa took quick aim with his flintlock and fired. The sound echoed wildly through the woods.

"You got 'im, Pa," Isaac yelled as he scampered off to retrieve their prize. He picked it up and started to run ahead, the dead rabbit dangling from his hand. Elizabeth hurried to catch up.

They finally arrived at Raccoon Run and the beginning of Big Flint. That was the name of Grandpa's land. Each family's property was named after the owner or after the nearest stream. Flint Billy was Grandpa's nickname.

"There's the cabin!" Elizabeth shouted.

Grandma and Grandpa were waiting on the porch. Elizabeth planted a kiss on Grandpa's cheek. Isaac followed his nose to Grandma's gingerbread, baking in the hearth.

But Pa announced that they should save the fun for suppertime. "We have to use what little daylight is left to find trees for Grandpa's baskets. C'mon, Isaac, grab your ax."

Pa and Isaac headed over the hill to where the best white oaks were growing. Grandpa called after them, "Make sure you find trees without knots! And remember, they should be straight as arrows."

Pa nodded and smiled. He was amused that after all these years Grandpa still thought only *he* knew which trees made good baskets.

They found several white oaks and began chopping. Dusk was creeping up on them as the sixth tree tumbled over.

"It's near dark, my boy," Pa said. "Grab ahold of that there small tree. I'll take this one. We'll come back in the morning for the others."

Elizabeth had spent a restful afternoon talking with Grandma as they strung sliced apples. Stringing fruits and vegetables was a way to preserve food. The garlands were hung out in the sunlight to dry. Then they were brought back inside to hang near the hearth until they were needed for a meal.

As they worked, Grandma told again the story of the Davis clan's journey from New Jersey to "north Western Virginny." Sometimes Elizabeth wished her family would move on farther west. But Grandma's tales of hardship on the trail made her grateful for the settled life she had been born into at Crooked Run.

Early the next morning, when Grandma wasn't looking, Elizabeth slipped out of the cabin to gather plants for Grandma's special remedies. Grandma should know how I've learned right well the different plants, barks, and berries, Elizabeth thought to herself.

Not far from the cabin, Elizabeth spotted a field of goldenrod and Joe-Pye weed. Farther on she found cherry bark and sassafras root. Soon her basket was overflowing.

SASSAFRAS ROOT
for spring tonic

GARLIC
for colds

COLTSFOOT
for chest colds

YARROW
for fever

POKEBERRY
for arthritis

CHERRY BARK
for cough syrup

Elizabeth knew Grandma Davis was the smartest person around when it came to making folks well. Grandma insisted that the good Lord wouldn't have wasted his time creating plants, or yarbs as she called them, if they weren't for some use. "It's up to us humans to figure out what they are for," Grandma always said.

Back at the cabin, Grandma had been looking all over for Elizabeth. But when she saw the brimming basket, Grandma broke into a big smile. Together they sorted the plants and tied them into bunches to dry in the shed behind the cabin. Then Grandma brewed a pot of special tea that was "good for the constitution." She poured a cup for Elizabeth.

Meanwhile, the men had gathered by the shed to split the fresh wood. Grandpa was directing, but Pa was doing much of the heavy work.

First, they split the logs, using iron wedges. "I shouldn't be stoopin' over so much," Grandpa said. "Blood rushes to my head and makes me dizzy."

Then, with a tool called a froe, they split the wood into thinner pieces. Next, Grandpa sat on the shaving horse. He removed the bark and shaved each piece evenly with a drawknife. "With you all doing the heavy work," he said, "I may just get caught up on my orders. Them there baskets take four days to make. When ya think about it, making a basket from a tree is somewhat of a miracle."

Next Grandpa split the pieces evenly until he had narrow strips. Finally, he shaved thin strips that would become the flexible splints for his baskets.

Now Grandpa nailed several splints to a board to form the bottom of the basket and to make a frame around which he could weave the sides.

"C'mon over, Elizabeth," Grandpa said, "and put your finger right here. Now hold tight while I get a couple of splints a-goin'. Time was when my fingers worked in ten different directions. Not so anymore." Grandpa sounded so sad that Elizabeth was doubly glad she was there to help.

A sturdy basket was an everyday necessity for a woman. It was practically an extension of her arm as she gathered eggs, carried food to the neighbors, or performed a dozen other tasks.

By late afternoon, Pa figured they had accomplished so much that he announced, "We best be heading home to Ma. If we hurry, we'll see Crooked Run 'fore dark."

It was almost pitch-black when the Davises sniffed the friendly smell of smoke from the cabin chimney drifting on the night air. The candlelit windows guided them to the cabin door, and Elizabeth and Isaac headed straight to their beds in the loft.

The next morning Pa, like always, hit the broomstick on the cabin ceiling to rattle Elizabeth and Isaac out of their beds. Reluctantly, they climbed down into the one-room cabin. Life at Crooked Run was back to normal—everyone working from sunup to sunset.

"Aunt Jane here's been up since 'fore dawn," Pa said, "doin' your chores, Elizabeth. This ain't no special day. Our trip to Grandpa is behind us. But since Bossie's been milked and the chickens fed, the day should feel special to you."

Pa winked as he finished his tirade. Elizabeth knew he wasn't really angry at her for sleeping late. After a hearty breakfast, she headed out to the yard to the jobs awaiting her.

Aunt Jane had filled the kettle with beef tallow that was melting over the hot flames. "Looks like we do the candle-dippin' first," Elizabeth said to Isaac. He gave her a disagreeable look, wishing for any other job. But the truth was that if they didn't make candles now, it would be a very dark winter. As they approached the kettle, Elizabeth held her nose in disgust at the rancid smell of the melting fat.

She and Isaac attached several wicks to a piece of wood so they could dip a number of candles at once. They had a competition to see who could make the thickest candles in the shortest time. Each candle had to be dipped at least twenty-five times, and dipping needed just the right touch. If the candles were in the hot wax more than a second, they would never build up because the wax from the previous dip would melt!

Today's job took them way past noon. But they had 120 candles to show for it.

After cleaning up the mess, Elizabeth was sent off to pull flax. The Davis family had a good crop this year. That meant Ma and Elizabeth could make lots of linen during the long winter days.

First, Elizabeth spent several hours carefully pulling the flax plant out of the ground by the root.

Then she tied the flax into bunches. For the next few days the flax would go through a dew-retting process—the morning and evening dew would soften the stems.

When Pa thought the flax was ready, he and Elizabeth would pull the dew-retted stems through a device called a hackle until the flax was in condition to be spun.

When all the flax had gone through the hackle, Ma could begin to spin it into thread. It would take weeks of spinning before Ma had enough to weave cloth. Then she would wait until Jud Smith came by with his loom.

What a treat it was to have new dresses, shirts, and pants! Mountain folk had only one change of clothes because it took so long to make cloth. Even when clothing wore out, the scraps were used for quilts and baby clothes. Nothing was ever discarded.

Meanwhile, Isaac was helping Pa hollow out a sycamore stump they had found in the woods. The stump would be made into a storage bin for food staples such as beans, peas, and corn.

First, Isaac collected dry oak shavings and stuffed them into the stump. Then Pa lit a fire inside, the flames shooting out like a big explosion.

Next Pa kicked the stump on its side and rolled it about the ground so that the entire inside would be softened. After the fire died down, Pa and Isaac would take turns scraping out the insides of the stump until it was a good size for storing food. Then they would make a tight cover to keep wild creatures out and the food safe inside.

A few days later Pa took Elizabeth and Isaac off to the town of New Salem to do errands. Although the Davises made all they could for themselves, certain items still had to be purchased. Money was almost nonexistent, so the Davis family would barter—exchange labor or goods—for what they needed.

Today Pa wanted Isaac to get nails for the new shed they were building. Isaac worked the bellows in the blacksmith's shop in return for the nails. Meanwhile, Elizabeth traded eggs and smoked pork with the townspeople for sugar and salt.

While the children were about their business, Pa paid a visit to the tavern. This was a general meeting place for men from surrounding parts. Here they could exchange local political news and pick up the mail, which was delivered to the tavern by a rider on horseback. Pa got a letter from his brother, Uncle Matthew, who had relocated a little farther north.

To Elizabeth's delight, Ely George, the itinerant peddler, was in town. He carried all sorts of treasures from the big city. The machine-made trinkets were her favorites, and Ely loved showing her his newest wares.

On the walk home, the children told Pa everything they had seen and heard. Elizabeth thought that life for New Salem folk sure looked easy compared with life in the holler.

Soon the days began to grow shorter, and cornfields in the hollers were begging to be harvested. Word went out that a workin', or harvesting, was planned for Saturday.

On Saturday morning, Pa and Isaac set out early to join the other harvesters at the Jacksons'. When that field was cleared, everyone would move on over to the Wilsons', then to Crooked Run, and finally end up at Grandpa's field. There the children would be waiting to play in the corn shock tepees. Harvest time was work *and* play for men, women, and children alike.

Several of Ma's friends stopped by to take Elizabeth to the harvest festival because Ma couldn't go this year. They carried along freshly slaughtered chickens and wild game, eggs, flour, sugar, apples, berries—anything that would make a grand supper following the workin'.

In Grandma's kitchen, the women sang "Barbara Allen" and other favorite tunes as they pared apples to make apple butter, chopped vegetables for rabbit stew, prepared squirrel meat for frying, and whipped up bowls of corn mush. Once the meal preparations were well under control, the ladies and girls moved into Grandma's living room for a quiltin'.

They had started the quilt last winter as a gift for bride-to-be Rebecca Randolph.

"She's a special one," Grandma kept repeating. "Is there anyone who works harder tendin' to the sick?"

Usually Elizabeth was allowed to do some quilting, but this one was too special for her inexperienced hands. Nevertheless, she loved listening to the conversation of the grown-ups. She also wondered who would catch the cat.

When a quilt for a bride was completed, a cat was placed in the center. The quilt was tossed up and down until the cat flew into someone's arms. The woman or girl who caught it was supposed to be married next. Elizabeth looked around at the unmarried ladies. She wished Aunt Jane could be there when the quilt was tossed. She'd make some man a fine wife.

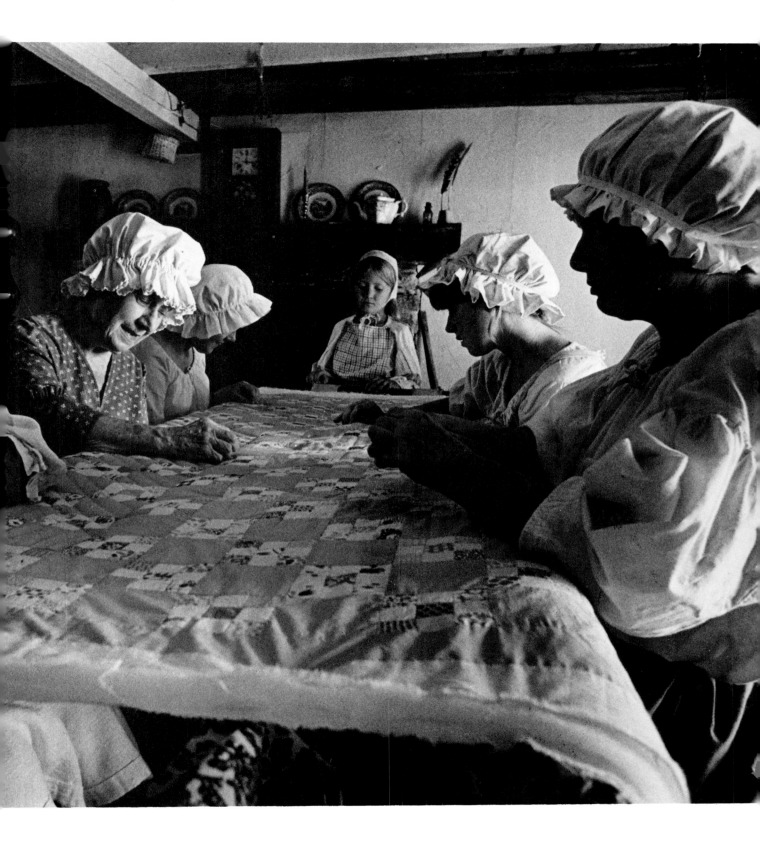

Just then the men arrived. The workin' was over, and they were ready to eat. But Pa called out, "Whoa, wait a minute, you young'ns. No feasting till the job is all done. Out by the shed is a mighty big pile of corn to be husked!"

With their stomachs growling, the young people sat in a circle and shucked as fast as they could. There was laughter and talk and general fun, especially when Ruth Wilson discovered that she was shucking the only red ear of corn. The young man or woman with the red ear got to kiss the person of his or her choice. Ruth held up the ear with a mischievous grin and gazed at Benjamin Evans.

Just as they started to kiss, someone clanged a pot from the kitchen announcing that supper was served.

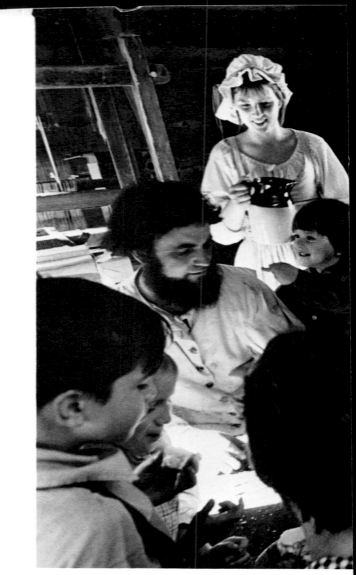

Some folks danced, while others sang, clapped their hands, or tapped their feet.

Elizabeth, Isaac, and the other children were too young for the dancing, so the women entertained them by helping them make corn husk dolls and corn husk fiddles with scraps left from the shucking.

Elizabeth soaked the husks in water so she could bend them any way she wanted. Then one of the women helped her shape a doll she could use as a bookmark for her Bible. Elizabeth draped a cape around the doll's shoulders and made long hair for her with corn silk.

Isaac tried to squeak out a tune on his new corn husk fiddle. One thing was for certain—a workin' was fun for everyone!

Now that the harvest was over, Elizabeth knew winter was on the way. Few noises would break the winter stillness at Crooked Run—just the cries of the newborn baby, Ma's gentle lullabies, or Pa's gunfire when he was lucky enough to find a deer.

The cold wind would swirl around the cabin, meaning no harm to the occupants inside. The sturdy little house at Crooked Run would keep the Davises secure and cozy the whole winter through.

Pa had followed Grandpa's advice: "Prepare for the worst, expect the best, and then take whatever comes." Now Elizabeth and her family could take a welcome rest from the toil of mountain life until the first signs of spring appeared outside the cabin door.

Our Thanks

During the time we were working on this book at Fort New Salem, we experienced "country"—a life-style that is chock-full of warmth, hospitality, down-home values, and mountain pride. We are extremely grateful to John Randolph, who founded and directs Fort New Salem, thereby enabling folks like us to know and feel the true character of Appalachia. We also thank Noel Tenney, Co-ordinator of Museum Education, for his hospitality on two separate occasions and for helping to make this book historically accurate.

We are especially grateful to George Pinkham, who played Pa. He created the spirit of the fictional Davis family, and without him we would not have had the wonderful location shots and special props. To the other interpreters—Sandy Godfrey, Amy Jo Pinkham, and Charlie Underwood, who completed the Davis family; Ireta Randolph, Fred Means, Shelba Zirkle, Connie Serrell, and little Jonathan Pinkham—we express our gratitude for their patience during the long hours of work. Much appreciation also goes to Paula Batson for the use of her farm and to Duke and Lillian Pinkham for their noonday meal and modern-day West Virginian hospitality.

Closer to home, we thank Jim Giblin and Ann Troy for their inspiration and painstaking interest in this project, and Adelia Geiger for getting the author to Fort New Salem on her first visit.

Joan Anderson & George Ancona

LOW CARB
EXPRESS

To my husband, Jonnie, and our
sons, Rothko and Louis x

An Hachette UK Company
www.hachette.co.uk

First published in Great Britain in 2018 by
Kyle Books, an imprint of Kyle Cathie Ltd
Carmelite House
50 Victoria Embankment
London, EC4Y 0DZ
www.kylebooks.co.uk

ISBN 978 0 85783 435 5

Project Editors: Kyle Cathie and Hannah Coughlin
Copy Editor: Stephanie Evans
Designer: Two Associates
Photographer: Con Poulos
Illustrator: Marie-Helene Jeeves
Food and Prop Stylist: Susie Theodorou
Production: Nic Jones and Gemma John

A Cataloguing in Publication record for this title is available
from the British Library.

10 9 8 7 6 5 4 3 2

Printed in China

**All nutritional data is per serving and excludes optional extras.
All eggs should be free-range.**

LOW CARB *EXPRESS*

CUT THE CARBS WITH
130 DELICIOUSLY HEALTHY RECIPES

ANNIE BELL

PHOTOGRAPHY BY CON POULOS

KYLE BOOKS

Contents

Noodles, Pasta and Pilafs

Protein Pots

Skinny Protein

Very Veggie

Sweet Satisfaction

Preface

Low carb is a giant umbrella of a term that underpins any number of branded diets – the Atkins, Dukan, South Beach and Banting are just a few that have become household names – and the principle is simple. In essence, the idea is to bump up your protein intake, eating fats, include some carbs with the emphasis on non-starchy fresh vegetables, and avoid processed foods and added sugars. And, in short, this approach works. Whether you are after an effective means of maintaining a stable weight, or are seeking to shed a few recalcitrant kilos, it can be readily tailored to suit you.

In addition, it is accessible. There is no need to carry a pair of microscales to calorie count, no recourse to special foods, it has the all-essential and elusive staying power. It is a way of eating that becomes second nature after a while, unlike so many 'diets' or 'regimes' that are so far removed from your comfort zone they have you looking for the nearest emergency exit. Any way of eating that is likely to work in the long-term has to fit in with your lifestyle, tastes, culture and health needs, and eating this way is endlessly adaptable. It is enjoyable and socially malleable.

But, being such a broad sweep, inevitably there are good low-carb diets and there are bad ones, healthy and unhealthy approaches. In the interim years since I wrote *Low Carb Revolution* I am guilty of having become a low carb geek. This started by returning to university to read a masters in human nutrition, which presented an opportunity to explore the science behind low-carb diets, and to gain an understanding about our metabolisms and how different foods affect us. I also wanted to understand more about the followers of such diets – their motivations, likes and dislikes, whether there are any trends that are common to every type of low-carb diet, and, finally, the optimum way of approaching this way of eating.

So this book is the distillation of that journey. I learned a great deal; in particular I was struck by how health conscious low-carb followers are. Considering that the key trends of a low-carb diet are to replace the starchy carbs, principally refined grains like pasta, white bread and rice, with non-starchy carbs such as green vegetables, aubergines, mushrooms and celeriac, and to reduce or omit added sugar, there is everything to recommend it. Low carb doesn't mean giving up grains entirely, but certainly rethinking how we include them: better quality whole grains served in smaller amounts with more fresh vegetables. While five a day, based on a total of 400 grams, may be the official recommendation for our veg intake, it is now known that the benefits of eating more increase incrementally above that figure. So the low-carb diet ticks another box, contributing to our need for dietary fibre, vitamins and minerals that can be lacking in refined carbohydrates.

In recent years healthy eating has preoccupied us like never before. Diets with no scientific evidence to support them come and go every year. We have seen so-called sugar-free diets that replace refined white sugar with honey, maple syrup and dates, low alkaline diets, detox diets, fermented food diets, clean eating, the list goes on, and there will always be some new fix around the corner. But if there is a holy grail of how to eat, then the Mediterranean Diet is widely regarded as offering the greatest health benefits and is linked to a lower incidence of heart disease, certain cancers and dementia. My design for a low-carb diet is tailored to reflect this diet, and the recipes that follow are similarly rich in vegetables, fruit, fish, legumes and extra virgin olive oil. For those that want a moderate lifestyle blueprint that really works, this is about as good as it gets.

Introduction

Blueprint for success

Ask a dietician, nutritionist or doctor the best way to lose weight, or stop gaining it, there is a strong chance they will tell you 'Eat less. Move more.' Simple. So why don't we? Why is it that so many people continue to struggle with their weight?

The reasons are complex; we are all different shapes, sizes, ages and our gender and genes all have a part to play, as do our hormones, our nervous system and our level of physical activity. Our genetic makeup especially plays a crucial role not only in determining our BMI or body mass index, which is used to determine whether we are a healthy weight (45-75% of individual variation is deemed hereditary), but in our eating behaviours and how we metabolise energy. It is also now known, for instance, that certain genetic mutations can lead to obesity. Undoubtedly in future an increased understanding of human genetics will lead to targeted interventions, including whether an individual will respond to particular dietary therapies or regimes. Perhaps in ten years time there will be a test to determine whether you are best suited to Intermittent Fasting (as popularised in the 5:2 diet), or to a low GI diet.

Added to our individual differences, we live in what is euphemistically known as an 'obesogenic environment'. In short, one that predisposes us to weight gain, and unfortunately at a time when our sedentary lifestyles mean that we need less energy than we used to. The 'smarter' life gets with its gizmos and gadgets, the less we need to get out of a chair. And there is no escaping that it is all too easy to eat more than we need. How hard it is to resist the temptation of the ready availability of high energy (for which read calorific) foods that call out from the high street every time we pop out, that can make it all but impossible to say 'no'. Why settle for just a *café latte* when you can have a warm chocolate fudge cookie to keep it company? Comfort eating too, another energy trap, the lure of a thick, buttery slice of cake or warming pud with ice cream is a downfall for many. Frequently, carrying a little extra weight is a slow and insidious creep of extra kilos that comes of too many occasional high energy treats, or being a little less active.

Satiety

But, aside from the many factors that can conspire to weight gain, for many the 'eat less' simply doesn't work because it means going hungry, and with that comes temptation. I believe that the key to the success of following a low-carb diet lies with satiety. This is the sense of feeling full after a meal that disinclines us to eat again, and moderates how much we eat on the next occasion. The principal trend of a low-carb diet is to replace starchy carbohydrates such as bread, pasta and rice with vegetables. This practice allows us to eat a much larger volume of food, as well as consuming more dietary fibre that helps to lower the energy density of the food in question. In short, you can eat more.

If you add in the second feature of a low-carb diet, to eat plenty of protein, this again leads to a sense of feeling well-nourished. While a food's palatability – its taste and texture – affects our sense of satiety, protein has the highest satiety index among the macronutrients (by weight for weight measured in calories), which is why it is pivotal to include even a small amount whenever you eat. Quite simply, protein reduces your appetite. It also has the highest thermogenic value, that is, the energy required in digesting it. In addition to meat and fish, eggs, dairy, legumes and nuts, seaweeds too are rich sources.

So it stands to reason that by consuming foods with a low energy density and plenty of fibre (veg), as well as those that are high on the satiety index (protein) you can eat well and still lose weight, without ever having to feel hungry. Low carb is not about calorie counting, which is not to say that you can't put on weight if you eat too much, but the general sense of feeling well-fed and nourished stop you from over-eating before that happens.

A word too about fats. All fats, both animal and vegetable sources, are high in energy, but as well as being crucial to our enjoyment of what we are eating, they play a role after we have eaten in keeping us full for longer by stimulating the production of the hormone cholecystokinin (known as CCK) which inclines us to stop eating. So while avoiding too many 'bad' fats, eating plenty of high quality fats that can be found in oily fish like salmon, in avocados, nuts, olive and rapeseed oil, as well as dairy, is a part of the picture.

Long-term well-being and weight loss

Feeling nourished leads to a sense of well-being, which is another key to success, particularly in the longer term. The joy of low-carb eating is the social inclusion – there is no need for it to be a solo journey or to call for radical behaviour change, which is really important. You remain a part of any gathering, because it fits in neatly with how you might feed your family and friends, and there will always be menu choices that will tick the box if you are eating out. Food is, after all, a source of enjoyment and sharing, and the wrong diet can lead to a sense of dejection leaving you feeling stressed, and hence you comfort eat and it becomes a vicious circle.

Short-term weight loss is comparatively easy and many diets will readily achieve that, but keeping the weight off is the hardest part. Adjusting or moderating your carbohydrate intake is something that will become second nature in the long-term. And it is a genuinely lovely way of eating, personally I cannot think of a more enjoyable day's grazing than

an abundance of vegetables and fruit, chicken and fish, a few nuts and legumes, and a little cheese or dairy. And not just those foods that someone else has decreed you should eat, but the ones that you personally want to eat. It is all about individualising how you eat in a way that fits in with your lifestyle. This flexibility is yet another key to its success.

How low is 'Low'?

The 'low' in low carb is something of a grey area, and while there are no officially recognised standards for Low Carbohydrate Diets, there has been some attempt to define them as follows (based on an adult on a nominal energy intake of 2,000 kcal a day):

Standard Diet: 250g carbohydrate per day (50% energy)

Moderate Carbohydrate Diet: 130-225g carbohydrate per day (26-45% energy)

Low Carbohydrate Diet: less than 130g carbohydrate per day (26% of energy)

Very Low Carbohydrate Diet (ketogenic): less than 30g carbohydrate per day (6% of energy)*

*Accurso et al, 2008

So, if you are trying to lose weight, reducing your carbohydrate intake to 100 grams or below should set the wheels in motion. But, if you are simply seeking to maintain your weight, then it may be possible to increase this.

Caution, however, applies to the extreme end of the scale and 'keto' diets. A ketogenic diet has long functioned as a medical intervention for the treatment of epilepsy, but, variations have also gained a mainstream following through the popularity of low-carbohydrate, high-fat rapid weight loss diets. Given the changes they effect in the way food is metabolised, these Very Low

Carbohydrate Diets are most safely followed under the guidance of a dietician. Basically you are placing your body in a state of artificial starvation, and this alters how you actually lose weight. Under normal circumstances you might expect to lose about 75 per cent fat and 25 per cent lean tissues – muscle, proteins and minerals – while during starvation losses of fat and lean tissue are about equal, as protein-rich tissue is broken down to provide glucose. On a pragmatic note, one of the risks of a 'keto' diet is rebound weight gain, as the body answers the stresses of perceived starvation with a determination to put down even more fat supplies than usual for that rainy day once you come off the diet, and there is a risk you will regain more than you lost.

The sugar family

Regardless of whether you are eating potatoes or bread, peas or broccoli, mangoes, avocado or yogurt, you will be eating sugar, and hence carbohydrate, of one type or another. Different foods contain different amounts, and following a low-carb diet is about lowering the total amount of sugars that you eat, to a level where you either maintain a stable weight, or lose it.

If we zoom in closer, carbohydrates consist of sugars, starches and fibres, and the main sugar is glucose, the monosaccharide (meaning single sugar) that hogs the podium: it is hard to over-estimate the role of glucose in our lives. We also know it as 'blood sugar', the instant energy for the body, the fuel that almost exclusively powers the brain. Glucose forms one of every two disaccharides (which are made up of two monosaccharides), and polysaccharides (made up of chains of monosaccharides) consist almost exclusively of this sugar. Fructose is the other key monosaccharide, the sweetest of the sugars that is found abundantly in fruit and honey. And there is a third single sugar galactose.

The names of the disaccharides, formed by two sugars, are again common enough to seem familiar. Sucrose accounts for table sugar, lactose is the sole carbohydrate or sugar to be found in milk, and then there is maltose which is principally produced during the fermentation process that results in alcohol, and by the body when starches are digested.

From here, in chemical terms, things get much more complicated. The polysaccharides, which consist of multiple sugars include glycogen, our body's storage of energy, also starches and fibres. Starches, which consist of hundreds and sometimes thousands of glucose molecules joined together, is how plants store energy. So starches in plants perform the same role as glycogen in humans. We find it in wheat, root crops, tubers such as potatoes and legumes including peas and beans. Basically we eat the plants, which are hydrolysed or broken down to glucose, which then provides us with energy. And finally there is fibre, which provides the structure to the plant in the form of its stems, roots, leaves and skin. As we only partially digest fibre, however, it contains about half the calories of the other carbohydrates. So the more of the plant we eat the better.

Good carbs, bad carbs

The poor little carb, many see it as the pariah in the deli to be avoided at all costs. Giving starchy carbs a wide berth has become synonymous with staying slim, a battle won by placing a curse on every grain of rice, strand of macaroni and chip in the land, and that's before we get to croissants and bread. What many people mean when they say they have 'given up' carbs, is that they don't eat starchy carbohydrates or the popular foods associated with them.

Starchy carbs, however, are only part of this large food group that we cannot live without. Carbohydrate is fuel, it is energy. Any food that is not protein or fat, is a carbohydrate. So they are to be found in vegetables, fruits and legumes in addition to grains or starchy carbohydrates, the genre with which the much-

maligned carbs have come to be associated. Milk also contains carbohydrate in the form of lactose. But all these foods contain differing amounts of carbohydrate, with non-starchy vegetables such as broccoli, green beans, aubergines and salads for instance, containing the least, and therefore these form the focus of a low-carb diet. Fruits too are non-starchy, but many still contain substantial amounts of sugar in the form of fructose, glucose and sucrose, and also need to be restricted.

Beyond the amount of carbohydrate or sugar that a food contains, there are also good and bad carbs, those that will benefit you, and those that won't. Table sugar, for instance, or that added to fizzy drinks and many processed foods, is energy without gain, it is the ultimate refined, concentrated 'bad' carb that brings only empty calories. Refined sugar has none of the vitamins, minerals and dietary fibre that are a part of fruit when you eat it whole. Instead, being concentrated, it is all too easy to eat more than you require in terms of your energy needs, and the sugar simply gets converted to fat.

And the same goes for refined starchy carbohydrates. Like table sugar, the 'refining' process, of grains in particular, strips them of the rich diversity of micronutrients and fibre and renders them as little more than calories with few nutritional benefits.

A healthy balance

It is easy to see why starchy carbs are shunned by those seeking to reduce their carbohydrate intake, given the amount they contain. But, exclusion of any food group brings with it risks of malnutrition at worst, or missing out on beneficial nutrients at the very least. And it is not so much the energy we require from starchy carbohydrates, as the fibre, vitamins and minerals. This is why quinoa, buckwheat, spelt and other 'unpolished' grains are of such value. To maximise our health we should ideally derive fibre from all its sources, vegetables, fruits, legumes and whole grains. By excluding grains we deprive

ourselves of a valuable source of insoluble fibre that is known to protect against bowel cancer.

It may be helpful to visualise carbohydrates as a pyramid. At the top we have whole grains, legumes, nuts and seeds, foods to be eaten in small quantities. In the middle, fruit, and vegetables such as beetroot and carrot that should be enjoyed in moderation, and at the base we have all the vegetables that are low in carbohydrates such as cauliflower, courgettes, broccoli and red peppers that are there to feast on whenever we are hungry.

Eating in this way offers us the best of both worlds; we lower our carbohydrate intake to a desirable level while benefiting from a varied intake of different foods. You don't need to eat large mounds of grains, just a few now and again will suffice. Nuts likewise; despite the temptation to dip into the cashew jar every time we put the kettle on, have maybe five unskinned almonds once a day or every other day, or a little chopped walnut scattered over a salad. Meanwhile, graze heartily on veg – use salad leaves as wraps, courgettes to make noodles, celery sticks and asparagus for dips, or aubergines as a toastie base, and you'll never feel you are missing out.

Processed sugar v sweeteners

The reduction of sugar in our diet is a hot topic, one that goes well beyond low-carb diets. 'Gratuitous' or added sugar, as found in fizzy drinks, confectionery, bakery goods, sweets and many ready meals is widely blamed, at least in part, for the growing incidence of obesity globally. And the majority of low-carb regimes will forego it altogether.

There are, however, alternative sweeteners that offer a way of minimising our intake of added sugars. The great divide in terms of trust is between the perception of sugars being natural or artificial. The latter are shrouded in distrust, even though to date there is no convincing evidence linking the likes of acedsulfame potassium (or Ace K), aspartame, saccharin and sucralose with diseases such as cancer and diabetes. Simply that for many people chemicals are an unacceptable substitute.

In practice, any food eaten in excess is likely to prove toxic at some point, and the levels at which these sweeteners are permitted are fractional in relation to the point at which that might prove an issue. That said, using natural ingredients has always been central to my recipes, and of late there have been two exciting developments for those with a sweet tooth. One is the introduction of stevia, a sweetener extracted from the leaves of a herb, *Stevia rebaudiana*, and also erythritol, a naturally occurring sugar alcohol derived from corn that has zero calories and no side-effects of note, and with which the better stevia products are blended. Stevia is only licensed in a highly refined form as a super-sweet extract, which has to be blended with bulking agents in order to render it suitable for use, and many of these are anything but natural. There are some excellent stevia products, but others are simply yesterday's chemicals in a new guise. The stevia erythritol blends such as Sukrin (which is GMO free) are so like granulated sugar, it is very hard to tell the difference between the two. So these are a welcome arrival.

If, however, if the call is simply for a half teaspoon or so of sugar to balance out the sharpness of a dressing, then there is little gain in using a substitute given the fractional carbohydrate value. The usefulness of alternative sweeteners lies more in sweet dishes where sugar might be added in quantity.

Snacking

Snacking is sometimes presented as the root of all evil. And there is a case in point, if in addition to having three square meals a day we add in lots of mini meals in between – not least if these take the form of convenience in the way of biscuits, cakes and crisps. So perhaps it is no surprise when dietary advice comes down on them heavily, by either limiting snacks or forbidding them altogether.

For some people (myself included), that's when the trouble begins, not least because any kind of restriction inevitably sets up a vicious cycle of denial and rewards, which leads to eating more and breaking the rules. Personally I don't like large meals, and I cannot bear feeling hungry. So, I eat when I feel like it, and that works for me.

Aside from trying to limit energy intake there is no logic in limiting snacks or suggesting a dietary regime. If you are someone who prefers to eat little and often rather than three times a day, a grazer for whom large meals are unappetising, you may even be placing yourself at an advantage. By avoiding the spikes in insulin that tend to occur if you eat big meals you achieve a steady supply of this hormone, that equates to eating a low glycaemic index diet, which relies on the slow release of sugars into the body and helps to stabilise blood sugar levels.

The ideal way of snacking is to eat a wide variety of foods, which is central to good nutrition. It's all about diversity, moderation and balance. So if snacking throughout the day is what works for you, there is no reason to change. By eating a little protein, this should help modify how much you eat at the next stage. Or, if you like, the amount you eat will average out over the course of a day.

Express

So far so perfect, if by reducing our carbs we can lose or maintain our ideal weight, not feel hungry and really enjoy eating and sharing food. But, in reality there are still challenges to pursuing a lifestyle of this type. And one of the greatest tests, that is the focus of this book, is our old friend 'time'. Given that about 75 per cent of bought prepared food contains added sugar, there is very little in the way of convenience for the low carber, which necessitates making it yourself. And fresh food requires preparation, as well as shopping and forethought.

So the aim of this book is to provide you with a collection of genuinely speedy recipes intended to help you stay on track with your best intentions. There are a small handful of recipes that run to 30 minutes, but the rest are 10, 15, 20 minutes. Genuinely express. It is amazing just how well we eat with even this little time at hand, and how diversely. The recipes that follow will take you from crispy pancetta on toasted almond bread, blinis with pea and avo smash and fried egg, tasty dips and pizza-style omelettes, to macaroni cheese fritters and bowls of noodles, little eats to graze on with a drink, and a silky raspberry and coconut ice cream or rich chocolate, date and orange mousse. So enjoy.

Breads, Pancakes, Muffins and Crackers

Walking past a bakery in the slipstream of warm yeasty air, without being lured into its comforting depths, requires superhuman levels of self-control if you happen to be avoiding the crumbs within. Bread is, without doubt, one of the hardest foods to relinquish if you are trying to reduce your starchy carb intake. And it's not just bakeries; everything to do with this genre that includes delights such as pancakes and blinis, focaccia smothered in cheese and olives, and crackers, are every bit as tempting. Even more so, if you happen to have given them up, when your finely tuned reward mechanism will be in full throttle.

But, providing you are open to a difference in character, instead of being resolute that the object of desire must be identical or a direct swap (AKA those sticklers for tradition among my immediate family), then there are some lovely alternatives that rely on ground nuts, coconut, soya and buckwheat flours and eggs. This makes them both richer in micronutrients and fibre than many standard breads and the like, and lower in carbs too. For the most part they are also rich in protein, and come with the bonus of sustaining you for that much longer than a refined bread. Equally, you are unlikely to want as much.

So, with the proviso of being open to a different style, the collection of recipes that follows is designed to see you through those essential starchy callings, whether you fancy a little something on toast or a bacon sarnie, a freshly baked muffin, smoked salmon blinis, or a wedge of focaccia. Many of these will also freeze well, which means if you happen to be on a solo mission but are trying to keep the remainder of your family and friends happy, you have the wherewithal to hand. Baked goods take no time at all to defrost.

I would still, however, treat these as an occasional indulgence. Not on account of their carb content; simply that they are concentrated foods, many contain nuts and it is easy to forget their energy status – not least given their oil content. So this needs to be factored into whatever else you are eating to achieve a healthy balance. But for those times when you are in cruise mode and trying to find a way through that doesn't involve half a baguette slathered with butter, it is good to know that any of these can be whisked up in a jiffy to occupy that space.

Coconut Almond Bread

This is my go-to loaf. With the texture of cornbread it is a tender and moist bread that can be wheeled out whenever the occasion calls for a slice, and whipped up at the speed of a muffin. Exceptionally nutritious, each slice translates to half an egg and a handful of almonds, and it sustains as readily as you might imagine.

MAKES 1 LOAF/16 SLICES

200g	ground almonds
40g	coconut flour
1½	teaspoons baking powder, sifted
⅓	teaspoon bicarbonate of soda, sifted
	large pinch of fine sea salt
7	large eggs
40g	coconut oil, melted, plus extra for greasing
1	generous tablespoon runny honey
1½	tablespoons cider vinegar
	golden linseeds, for dusting (optional)

Preheat the oven to 170°C fan/190°C electric/gas mark 5. Combine the ground almonds, coconut flour, baking powder, bicarb and salt in a large bowl. Whisk the remaining wet ingredients together in another large bowl, then pour these over the dry ingredients and beat or whisk until smooth.

Liberally grease a 450g non-stick loaf tin with melted coconut oil, transfer the mixture to the tin, smoothing the top, dust with seeds, if wished, and bake for 35–40 minutes until golden and shrinking from the sides. Run a knife around the edge and turn out onto a wire rack or board to cool, standing the loaf the right way up.

ENERGY KCAL	CARBOHYDRATE G	SUGARS G	PROTEIN G	FAT G	SATURATED FAT G	SALT G
151	2.6	1.7	6.5	12.2	3.7	0.3

Crispy Pancetta on Almond Bread

SERVES 2

8	slices smoked pancetta (approx. 75g)
approx. 2	teaspoons softened unsalted butter
2	slices Coconut Almond Bread (see above)
	cholula (hot sauce)

Preheat the grill. Lay out the pancetta rashers without touching in a roasting or grill pan. Grill the top side briefly until golden and ruched, then turn and very briefly grill the other side. Drain the rashers on a double thickness of kitchen paper.

Butter the bread, lay the crispy pancetta on top, and splash with cholula sauce.

ENERGY KCAL	CARBOHYDRATE G	SUGARS G	PROTEIN G	FAT G	SATURATED FAT G	SALT G
245	0.2	0.1	7.4	23.8	10.2	1.8

Swiss Chard Bruschettas with Chilli and Garlic

Hard to believe that greens on toast can be quite so tasty – a good use for young and tender chard or, that johnny-come-lately among greens, the humble kale, should you be able to buy it by the bunch rather than ready sliced.

MAKES 4

200–250g	young rainbow chard, stalks trimmed and sliced 1cm thick, leaves thickly sliced
approx. 4	tablespoons extra virgin olive oil
1	teaspoon finely sliced medium-hot red chilli
2	garlic cloves, peeled and finely sliced
	sea salt
4	thick slices Coconut Almond Bread (see page 18)
20g	finely shaved Parmesan
	lemon wedges, to serve

Bring a large pan of salted water to the boil. Add the chard stalks, cook for 1 minute and then add the leaves and cook for a further 2 minutes. Drain into a colander and press out any excess water – a potato masher is good for this.

Heat a tablespoon of oil in a large non-stick frying pan over a medium heat, add the chilli and garlic and fry briefly until fragrant and sizzling. Add the chard, season with salt and heat through, turning it a few times.

Toast the bread (you may find this easiest under the grill), arrange on four plates, drizzle with a little oil and spread over the greens, then drizzle with a little more oil and scatter with Parmesan shavings. Accompany with lemon wedges to squeeze over.

ENERGY KCAL	CARBOHYDRATE G	SUGARS G	PROTEIN G	FAT G	SATURATED FAT G	SALT G
149	1.8	0.4	2.9	14.1	2.8	0.4

Sesame Parmesan Crackers

I am happy to give the vast majority of crackers a wide berth – unless, that is, they come laced with Parmesan, which is rarely better than when it is toasted. Add some sesame or poppy seeds into the equation, and it gets even harder to pass them up. These make a great snack, either on their own with a drink, in lieu of a pastry base for canapés, or for dipping (see page 35).

MAKES 24–30 MINI TRIANGLES/SERVES 6

90g	ground almonds
25g	freshly grated Parmesan
1	tablespoon sesame seeds
	large pinch of sea salt
	knife tip of cayenne pepper
approx. ½	medium egg white

Preheat the oven to 160°C fan/180°C electric/gas mark 4. Combine all the dry ingredients in a medium bowl and add just enough egg white to bring the mixture together into a dough.

Lay a sheet of clingfilm a little larger than a non-stick baking sheet on the worktop. Place the dough on top, then cover it with a sheet of baking paper the size of the baking sheet and press the dough flat using your hands, before rolling it into a wafer-thin (1–2mm) circle about 23cm in diameter. Place the baking sheet on top, upside down, and by wrapping the excess clingfilm over the sides invert the rolled dough onto the baking sheet. Peel off the clingfilm, leaving it on the baking paper. Cut the dough into 5cm squares and then halve these into triangles – I find a pizza cutter the best tool for this. You can also bake the crackers in a single sheet and break it up once cooked.

Bake for 15–20 minutes until lightly golden; you may need to turn the tray around halfway through if the crackers are colouring unevenly. Leave to cool before carefully lifting them off the paper. These should keep well in a covered container for several days.

ENERGY KCAL	CARBOHYDRATE G	SUGARS G	PROTEIN G	FAT G	SATURATED FAT G	SALT G
129	1.0	0.6	5.4	11.0	1.7	0.1

Buckwheat Blinis

A tender, puffed blini warm from the pan, adorned with a sliver of smoked salmon, a smidgen of soured cream and a spoonful of salmon roe is as hard to contemplate eschewing as a bacon sandwich or BLT (see page 60). The best blinis are made with buckwheat flour, for that delicate sourness and texture that cannot be replicated. Conveniently, this pseudograin is high in both fibre and protein, while the addition of a little soya flour takes care of the remainder. Blinis have any number of other roles to play in lieu of a slice of toast, and they are 'express'. A stack of these in the fridge that can be briefly rewarmed in a frying pan will be ever handy.

MAKES APPROX. 16/SERVES 8

40g	buckwheat flour
15g	soya flour
	pinch of sea salt
2	medium eggs, separated
130 ml	skimmed milk
25g	unsalted butter, plus a knob

Put the buckwheat and soya flours and salt in a large bowl, add the egg yolks and then gradually start to blend in the milk, whisking until smooth. Melt and add 25g of the butter, then whisk the egg whites until stiff in a medium bowl using an electric whisk, and fold them into the batter mixture.

Heat a large, non-stick frying pan for several minutes over a medium heat, add a knob of butter to start the blinis off, and drop three heaped tablespoons of the mixture into the pan to give you three pancakes, each about 8cm in diameter. Cook for 1½ minutes until golden on the underside (you may find a couple of bubbles breaking on the surface too), then turn and cook for a further 30–60 seconds until golden on the other side. Transfer them to a plate and repeat with the remaining batter; there should be no need to add any further butter to the pan. You should have 15–16 blinis at the end.

ENERGY KCAL	CARBOHYDRATE G	SUGARS G	PROTEIN G	FAT G	SATURATED FAT G	SALT G
84	4.6	1.0	3.7	5.5	2.7	0.1

Blinis with Smoked Salmon

I find a couple of these mid-morning, if I'm on my own, is a fine way of lifting my spirits, they ever evoke that party spirit. Although that coveted teaspoon of salmon roe just might have to wait.

PER PERSON

30g	smoked salmon
2	warm Blinis (see above)
1	heaped teaspoon soured cream
1	teaspoon salmon roe (optional)
½	teaspoon finely chopped dill
	lemon slices, to serve

Pile the smoked salmon onto the blinis, dollop with the soured cream, then the salmon roe, if including, and scatter with dill. Accompany with lemon.

ENERGY KCAL	CARBOHYDRATE G	SUGARS G	PROTEIN G	FAT G	SATURATED FAT G	SALT G
90	0.7	0.6	7.2	6.5	2.7	0.9

Smoked Ham and Camembert Muffins

Like so many of the most alluring low-carb breakfasts, these rely on eggs, cheese and ham, which, together with almonds, makes them little powerhouses of goodness. Just one will make for a deliciously savoury breakfast or brunch, at the ready if you have baked them a day in advance, and even better if they happen to be warm.

MAKES 16–18 MUFFINS

40g	unsalted butter, melted, plus extra for greasing the moulds
200g	ground almonds
40g	freshly grated Parmesan
⅓	teaspoon baking powder, sifted
1½	teaspoons bicarbonate of soda, sifted
	large pinch of fine sea salt
8	medium eggs
1	generous tablespoon runny honey
1½	tablespoons cider vinegar
150g	sliced smoked ham, cut into 1cm dice
	a generous ¼ of a Camembert, cut into thin segments, halved across

Preheat the oven to 170°C fan/190°C electric/gas mark 5 and arrange 16–18 silicone muffin cases in a couple of muffin tins (or use paper wrappers, in which case, brush them with melted butter).

Combine the ground almonds, Parmesan, baking powder, bicarb and salt in a large bowl. Whisk the remaining wet ingredients together in another large bowl, then pour these over the dry ingredients and beat or whisk until smooth. Fold in the ham.

Fill the moulds by two-thirds. Drop a sliver of Camembert into the centre of each one and bake for 20–23 minutes until risen and crusty. Transfer to a wire rack and leave to cool, then unmould. They will be delicious for a couple of days, if stored loosely covered. They also freeze well.

ENERGY KCAL	CARBOHYDRATE G	SUGARS G	PROTEIN G	FAT G	SATURATED FAT G	SALT G
172	1.9	1.5	9.5	13.7	3.9	0.6

Fake-accia Base

This is something like a nutty soda bread, both delicate and tender. Come suppertime, I find if I place one of these centrally on the table, by the end, sliver after sliver will have been carved off and there will be little or nothing left. With a blend of linseeds and almonds, it also packs a punch nutritionally, broadening out the range of fibre that you will be getting from your daily intake of vegetables, fruit and legumes. Just don't call it a focaccia or a pizza – this is delicious in its own right, and vive la différence. *And, like a pizza base, you can dress it up in endless ways.*

Flaxseeds and linseeds are one and the same thing; here it is yellow seeds you want, which are milder and sweeter than the brown. This will probably mean grinding your own. I cannot praise these little seeds highly enough, for both their fibre content (it contains both soluble and insoluble fibre) and for being one of the richest sources of the essential omega 3 alpha-linolenic fatty acid.

MAKES 1 X 20CM FAKE-ACCIA BASE

50g	ground yellow linseeds
50g	ground almonds
	pinch of Maldon sea salt
1	heaped tablespoon soya flour
1	rounded teaspoon baking powder
2	medium eggs

Preheat the oven to 220°C fan/240°C electric/gas mark 9 with a non-stick baking sheet inside. Combine the ground linseeds, ground almonds and salt in a large bowl. Sift over and mix in the soya flour and baking powder. In a medium bowl, whisk the eggs with 75ml of water until thoroughly blended. Add to the dry ingredients and stir to blend. Leave the mixture to stand for 5 minutes, during which time it will thicken up.

Without stirring, tip the dough onto a sheet of baking paper about the size of the baking sheet, lay a sheet of clingfilm over the top and use your fingers to gently spread it into a circle about 20cm in diameter and 1cm thick. Tidy the edge, again using your fingers, then peel off the clingfilm. Proceed to dress the base (see pages 27–28).

FOR NUTRITIONAL DATA SEE PAGE 27 AND 28

Rosemary Fake-accia

As bread goes it doesn't get any simpler, and with its rustic charm, this makes for the perfect accompaniment to a bowl of soup. Rosemary is a pungent herb and a little goes a long way, so if the needles are attached as sprigs at the base, cut this off to separate them before scattering over the fake-accia.

SERVES 6

1	fake-accia base (see page 26)
¼	tablespoon rosemary needles
⅓	teaspoon Maldon sea salt
2	tablespoons extra virgin olive oil

When preparing the base, before removing the sheet of clingfilm, make indentations in the dough about 2cm apart, using a finger. Remove the clingfilm. Scatter over the rosemary needles and the salt, and drizzle over a tablespoon of oil.

Slide the baking paper onto the hot baking sheet and bake for 12–15 minutes until golden and risen. Drizzle another tablespoon of oil over the fake-accia. Use a spatula to loosen the fake-accia and slip it onto a board before cutting. Eat warm or at room temperature.

ENERGY KCAL	CARBOHYDRATE G	SUGARS G	PROTEIN G	FAT G	SATURATED FAT G	SALT G
172	1.2	0.6	6.6	14.7	1.8	0.4

Red Pepper, Feta and Olive Fake-accia

With toasted cheese, roast peppers, olives and tomatoes, this is pizza-esque in its appeal, and like most focaccias has a thick, bread base. It's great for eating with your hands once it is cold.

SERVES 6

1	fake-accia base (see page 26)
100g	cherry tomatoes, halved
100g	roast red peppers, cut into thin strips
	small handful of rocket leaves
50g	feta, coarsely crumbled
30g	pitted black olives, halved
1	tablespoon extra virgin olive oil

Slide the prepared base on the paper onto the hot baking sheet, and bake for 10 minutes until lightly golden. About halfway through this time prepare the topping ingredients. Toss the cherry tomatoes, peppers and rocket together in a medium bowl – assuming you are drawing on a jar of roast peppers in oil, there should be no need to add any extra, but if you have roasted your own peppers, then coat everything in a drizzle of oil. Scatter these over the baked dough, then the feta and olives and drizzle all over with oil, including the crust.

Bake for a further 10–12 minutes until tinged with gold and toasty at the edges. Leave to cool to room temperature. Use a spatula to loosen the fake-accia and slip it onto a board before cutting.

ENERGY KCAL	CARBOHYDRATE G	SUGARS G	PROTEIN G	FAT G	SATURATED FAT G	SALT G
191	2.4	1.7	8.3	15.5	2.8	0.8

Baked Apple Custard Cakes

These little baked custard cakes are golden and delicately crispy at the edges, with just enough sweetness to take the edge off a sugar craving. Soya flour is high in protein and low in carbs, which keeps these well within the remit.

MAKES APPROX. 9 CAKES/SERVES 4

approx. 1	tablespoon vegetable oil
30g	soya flour
1	medium egg
150ml	whole milk
	pinch of sea salt
2	heaped teaspoons granulated stevia (i.e. equivalent to 2 heaped teaspoons sugar)
½	eating apple, peeled, quartered, cored and thinly sliced across, end slices discarded
10g	salted butter
2	teaspoons dark rum (optional)
	soured cream, to serve (optional)

Preheat the oven to 220°C fan/240°C electric/gas mark 9. Drizzle ½ teaspoon of oil into 9 holes in a fairy cake tin and place in the oven for 10 minutes. Meanwhile, whizz the soya flour, egg, milk, salt and stevia in a blender, then scrape the sides and whizz again.

Half-fill the hot moulds with the batter, then drop a couple of apple slices into the centre of each one and dot with a nib of butter, and bake for 15–20 minutes until risen and golden.

Drizzle a few drops of rum over each little cake, if wished. Leave to stand for about 5 minutes before loosening and eating warm, with soured cream, if wished. They can also be reheated for 5 minutes at 160°C fan/180°C electric/gas mark 4.

ENERGY KCAL	CARBOHYDRATE G	SUGARS G	PROTEIN G	FAT G	SATURATED FAT G	SALT G
134	5.6	4.5	6.0	9.3	2.8	0.1

Carrot Cake Muffins

These take the succulence of a carrot cake to its logical extreme – half-muffin, half-pudding – with all the character we love in this genre of cake in the way of cinnamon, nuts and raisins. As with the Smoked Ham and Camembert Muffins (see page 25), they also make a handy all-in-one breakfast.

MAKES APPROX. 8 MUFFINS

2	medium eggs
40g	quark
1	tablespoon granulated stevia (i.e. equivalent to 1 tablespoon sugar)
1	teaspoon ground cinnamon
	pinch of sea salt
50g	ground almonds
1	rounded teaspoon baking powder, sifted
1	rounded teaspoon cornflour, sifted
150g	grated carrot*
30g	raisins
25g	pine nuts, plus 1 tablespoon
	squeeze of lemon juice

Preheat the oven to 180°C fan/200°C electric/gas mark 6 and arrange 8 silicone muffin cases in a muffin tin. Whisk the eggs, quark, stevia, cinnamon and salt in a large bowl. Whisk in the ground almonds, fold in the baking powder and cornflour, then fold in the carrot, raisins, 25g of pine nuts and a squeeze of lemon juice. Fill the moulds by two-thirds to three-quarters, scatter over the remaining pine nuts and bake for 20 minutes until golden and risen. Pop the muffins out of their moulds and leave to cool on a wire rack for 10 minutes if you want to eat them warm, or leave to cool completely. These will still be good the following day, if loosely covered.

* There is no need to peel the carrots as the skin adds flavour and is a great source of fibre. Just give them a good scrub before grating.

ENERGY KCAL	CARBOHYDRATE G	SUGARS G	PROTEIN G	FAT G	SATURATED FAT G	SALT G
114	5.9	4.5	4.7	7.5	0.8	0.2

Dipping and Dolloping

If dips were garments they would be that go-to pair of jeans that never lets you down. Except that is, at party-time. I know that we try to prepare dips for an occasion with a little chopped parsley or dusting of cayenne pepper and drizzle of oil, but they are what they are. And it is hard to over-estimate their potential role in providing a ready snack with crudités at times when a slice of toast or packet of crisps might seem the obvious choice.

Despite being the meeters and greeters of the chill cabinet as you enter the supermarket, there is every reason to make your own. A brief peruse of the bottom-of-tub ingredient list doesn't make pretty reading; the majority of bought-in dips are anything but nutritious with excessive amounts of fat, salt, preservatives and flavourings. The best are simple and tasty, nothing fancy, just a handful of ingredients. Many of my favourites rely on the convenience of a tin of sardines or tuna, some smoked salmon or mackerel, which are the perfect way to take the edge off your appetite between meals without resorting to a sandwich. Or, if it is a light vegetable-based dip, then some quail eggs or prawns again tick the box of getting in a little protein, which is so important to that feeling of being replete.

The ideal is to eat a rainbow of vegetables, so dip into as many colour bands as possible. Aside from being low in carbs, this is the best possible way of getting the optimum variety of phytonutrients, which behave as antioxidants and mop up damaging free radicals. Every colour has something different to offer in protecting us against disease risks. So mix it up and graze on the full spectrum:

Red
Red peppers – cut into long strips
Radishes – trimmed
Beetroot – cut into fine wedges
Red cherry tomatoes

Yellow
Yellow peppers – cut into long strips
Yellow cherry tomatoes
Yellow patty pan squash – sliced
Yellow bobby beans – stalk-ends trimmed and
   boiled for 3–4 minutes, drained and cooled,
   or steamed

White
Cauliflower – florets
Button mushrooms – stalks trimmed
Endive – separated into leaves
Mouli radish – peeled and sliced
White asparagus – peeled and steamed or boiled
   for 8–30 minutes depending on thickness

Orange
Orange peppers – cut into long strips
Orange cherry tomatoes
Carrots – trimmed, peeled and cut into batons

Green
Green peppers – cut into long strips
Cucumber – sliced or cut into batons
Little Gem leaves – the smaller the better
Sugarsnaps or mangetout – raw or blanched
Celery – inner sticks of heart
Green beans – stalk-ends trimmed and boiled for
   3–4 minutes, drained and cooled, or steamed
Long-stem broccoli – trimmed and boiled for
   4–5 minutes, drained and cooled
Asparagus spears – trimmed and boiled for
   3–5 minutes, drained and cooled

Muhammara

Overwhelmed by the increasing mountain of walnuts growing in our garden, and eager to use them, this dip came to the rescue. The bitterness of walnuts spars particularly well with the sweetness of peppers, but any unroasted nuts would work. Ready-shelled nuts and jars of roast peppers make this infinitely speedier. The ideal peppers are only lightly vinegared and seasoned with salt. The Sesame Parmesan Crackers (see page 21) are lovely with both dips.

SERVES 6

100g	shelled walnuts
1	teaspoon finely chopped medium-hot red chilli
¼	garlic clove, peeled
1 x 300g	jar roast peppers (e.g. Sacla), drained
½	teaspoon honey
1	level teaspoon ground cumin
2	tablespoons extra virgin olive oil, plus extra to serve
	finely chopped flat-leaf parsley, to serve

Put the walnuts, chilli and garlic in a food processor and whizz to a crumb-like consistency, without reducing them to a paste. Transfer this to a medium bowl. Add the peppers, honey and cumin to the food processor and reduce to a purée, then add the olive oil. Add this to the nuts and blend. Transfer to one or two shallow bowls. Drizzle over a little more oil and scatter with parsley. Cover and chill until required. It will keep for several days.

ENERGY KCAL	CARBOHYDRATE G	SUGARS G	PROTEIN G	FAT G	SATURATED FAT G	SALT G
181	5.3	5.0	3.4	15.8	15.9	0.0

Soured Cream and Chive Dip

Realising with some shame the amount of ready-made tubs of this dip we were getting through in our house, the challenge was on to devise a speedy equivalent. This is high in protein and low in fat, unlike shop bought ones that come loaded with sugar and fat. But, the texture is every bit as silky. It is particularly good with boiled quail eggs and cooked prawns.

SERVES 6

250g	quark
75g	soured cream
½	teaspoon caster sugar
	sea salt
2	teaspoons lemon juice
1	heaped tablespoon finely chopped chives

Whizz the quark and soured cream in a food processor until smooth, then add the sugar, a little salt and the lemon juice and whizz to blend. Add the chives and give the dip another quick whizz. Taste for seasoning and add a little more salt, if necessary. Scoop into a small bowl, cover and chill until required. It will keep well for a couple of days.

ENERGY KCAL	CARBOHYDRATE G	SUGARS G	PROTEIN G	FAT G	SATURATED FAT G	SALT G
64	2.5	2.4	6.3	3.1	1.9	0.1

Avocado and Coconut Dip

If you can have too much of a good thing, then guacamole is guilty of luring us in its direction every time an avocado in the fruit bowl feels softly yielding and ripe. This is a variation on that theme, but with Asian tones it slots neatly into any line-up of curries and spicy ensembles, as well as being lovely to eat with crudités. Some finely sliced baby courgettes scattered over will add some extra crunch.

SERVES 4

juice of ½–1 lime

flesh of 2 avocados (approx. 200g)

1 heaped tablespoon coconut yogurt

½ teaspoon ground cumin

1 spring onion, trimmed and sliced

small handful of coriander, plus a little extra, chopped, to serve

sea salt

cayenne pepper

Adding the juice of just ½ lime, whizz all the ingredients to a smooth purée in a food processor. Taste for seasoning and add a little more lime, if necessary. Transfer to a serving bowl, dust with a little more cayenne pepper and scatter over a little extra chopped coriander. Cover and chill until required. It should keep well for up to a day.

ENERGY KCAL	CARBOHYDRATE G	SUGARS G	PROTEIN G	FAT G	SATURATED FAT G	SALT G
115	0.8	0.6	1.3	11.3	3.3	trace

Courgette Dip with Coconut, Lime and Mint

It is rare to encounter a dip with quite such a squeaky clean profile. Bravo to courgettes, one of my all-time favourite veggies, particularly when roasted, which concentrates their flavour and natural sweetness. Courgettes also possess the curious talent of firming up on cooling, which is more than a little handy when making a dip. This is fab with everything from olives to salami and crudités.

SERVES 6

800–900g	courgettes, ends trimmed and thickly sliced
2	tablespoons coconut oil, melted
	sea salt, black pepper
	juice of ½–1 lime
1	heaped teaspoon dried mint
	few tiny mint leaves (optional)

Preheat the oven to 220°C fan/240°C electric/gas mark 9. Arrange the courgettes in a crowded layer in a large roasting pan, drizzle over the coconut oil and toss, then season with salt and pepper. Roast for 20 minutes, stirring halfway. It will be darker on the base than on top, so don't be tempted to cook them for longer.

Tip the courgettes into a food processor, leaving behind any liquid given out on cooking, and reduce to a purée. Add the juice of ½ lime and the mint and whizz again, then taste for seasoning, and add a little more lime juice, if necessary. Transfer the dip to a bowl, leave to cool, then cover and chill before adorning with a few tiny mint leaves, if wished. It should keep well for several days.

ENERGY KCAL	CARBOHYDRATE G	SUGARS G	PROTEIN G	FAT G	SATURATED FAT G	SALT G
74	2.7	2.7	2.7	5.1	4.0	0.0

Green Papaya, Cinnamon and Cashew Salsa

Pomegranate molasses, cinnamon and mint give hints of the Middle East, while the cashews are creamy and aromatic. The papaya should be on the under-ripe side, so the dice remain firm. This is good with griddled lamb steaks and chops, seared pork fillet or ham hock.

SERVES 6

50g	unroasted cashews, coarsely chopped
2	spring onions, trimmed and finely sliced
2	tablespoons avocado oil
2	teaspoons pomegranate molasses
⅓	teaspoon ground cinnamon
2	tablespoons finely chopped mint
	sea salt
	squeeze of lemon juice
1	green papaya, skinned, halved and deseeded, cut into 1cm dice

Combine the cashews and onions in a medium serving bowl and dress with the oil and pomegranate molasses. Stir in the cinnamon and mint, and season with salt and a squeeze of lemon juice. Very gently stir in the papaya. Cover and chill for up to a couple of hours.

ENERGY KCAL	CARBOHYDRATE G	SUGARS G	PROTEIN G	FAT G	SATURATED FAT G	SALT G
116	6.2	2.4	2.3	8.8	1.3	trace

Melon, Lime and Coriander Salsa

You may not be old enough to remember the trend for serving shellfish with tropical fruits – crab with mango and the like – which, when it was bad was truly terrible, but, when it was good, could be sensational. This discreetly sweet and sharp salsa with a hint of chilli and its delicate perfume makes it the perfect aside to fish. In terms of dipping and dolloping it would be hard to beat some cooked prawns of a certain size or crispy pan-fried salmon.

SERVES 4

1	tablespoon lime juice
	sea salt
2	tablespoons extra virgin olive oil
2	tablespoons finely chopped red onion
1	tablespoon finely chopped medium-hot red chilli
200g	melon flesh, cut into 1cm dice
	large handful of finely chopped coriander

Whisk the lime juice with a little salt in a medium bowl, then stir in the olive oil, and add the onion and chilli. You can prepare the salsa to this point well in advance, in which case cover and set aside.

Just before serving, stir the melon and coriander into the dressing.

ENERGY KCAL	CARBOHYDRATE G	SUGARS G	PROTEIN G	FAT G	SATURATED FAT G	SALT G
77	3.3	3.2	0.5	6.4	0.9	trace

Avocado, Cashew and Mint Guacamole

Another dip that draws on guacamole's generous spirit for reinvention, here with mint, avocado oil and cashews for both their scent and the texture. Any roast nut works a treat: almonds are lovely, and pistachios too if you are not averse to shelling them.

SERVES 4

25g	roast cashews, plus a few extra, finely chopped, to serve
	flesh of 2 avocados (approx. 200g)
	handful of mint leaves
½	teaspoon coarsely chopped medium-hot red chilli
½	spring onion (bulb section), trimmed and thickly sliced
1½	tablespoons avocado oil, plus a little extra to serve
1	tablespoon lime juice, plus extra to serve
	sea salt

Chop the cashews in a food processor as finely as possible. Add all the remaining ingredients and whizz to a paste, flecked with the flavouring ingredients. Spoon it into a small bowl, drizzle over a little avocado oil and a squeeze of lime juice, and scatter over a few finely chopped nuts.

Cover and chill until required. It should keep well for up to a day.

ENERGY KCAL	CARBOHYDRATE G	SUGARS G	PROTEIN G	FAT G	SATURATED FAT G	SALT G
183	1.6	0.7	2.6	17.9	3.2	0.1

Creamy Goat's Cheese

This dip makes a virtue out of a chèvre log – deliciously aromatic without being overly pungent. It has the consistency of cream cheese, but with a fraction of the fat and more character. A mix of fromage frais and soured cream would also work well and be a little richer. Some chopped chives stirred through would not go amiss either. It certainly won't shame you dressed for the party with an astute selection of young crisp spring veg for dipping – thin carrot and celery batons, lettuce heart leaves, trimmed radishes – some Parma ham too goes especially well.

SERVES 4

150g	medium-mature goat's cheese (e.g. chèvre log), rind discarded, and diced (about 120g without the rind)
100g	low-fat fromage frais
	black pepper
	extra virgin olive oil, to serve

Whizz the goat's cheese, fromage frais and a little black pepper in a food processor until creamy. Scoop into a small serving dish, drizzle over a little oil, cover and chill until required. The dip will keep well for several days.

ENERGY KCAL	CARBOHYDRATE G	SUGARS G	PROTEIN G	FAT G	SATURATED FAT G	SALT G
117	1.4	1.3	8.1	8.8	5.5	0.5

Smoked Salmon and Dill Mousse

In the absence of butter, which is a mainstay in most smoked salmon pâtés, this is lighter and more like a mousse. It's a great basic; you can use it to fill little lettuce leaves or slather it on halved boiled eggs. It is also hard to beat warm Buckwheat Blinis (see page 22) as a plinth. Spoon a mound of the mousse in the centre of each one, and, if wished, top with a little salmon caviar and scatter with finely chopped chives.

SERVES 6

100g	smoked salmon
25g	soured cream
125g	low-fat fromage frais
1	tablespoon lemon juice
1	teaspoon chopped shallot
1	tablespoon chopped dill, plus extra to serve
	black pepper

Whizz the smoked salmon, soured cream and fromage frais to a smooth paste in a food processor, then incorporate the lemon juice. Add the shallot, dill and black pepper, and continue to whizz until the herbs are very finely chopped. Pack the mousse into a bowl or jar and scatter over a little extra dill, either cover or close, then chill. It will keep well for several days.

ENERGY KCAL	CARBOHYDRATE G	SUGARS G	PROTEIN G	FAT G	SATURATED FAT G	SALT G
52	1.2	1.1	5.5	2.8	1.0	0.5

Smoked Mackerel Pâté

This pâté lends itself to being slathered over a slice of toasted Coconut Almond Bread (see page 18) with thinly sliced radishes and salad sprouts, and is also great with a poached egg popped on top or with crudités. It provides all-essential omega-3, plus it's high in protein and comparatively low in fat for a dip of this type.

SERVES 4

150g	smoked mackerel fillets, skinned
1	teaspoon chopped shallot
100g	quark
50g	soured cream
1	tablespoon lemon juice
	cayenne pepper

Whizz all the ingredients, including a little cayenne pepper, to a paste in a food processor, then mound into a small serving dish, or small bowls. Dust with a little more cayenne pepper. Cover and chill until required. It will be good for a couple of days.

ENERGY KCAL	CARBOHYDRATE G	SUGARS G	PROTEIN G	FAT G	SATURATED FAT G	SALT G
163	1.5	1.4	11.8	12.1	3.8	0.7

Sardine Gribiche

The choice of canned fish in supermarkets has grown to include some finer brands that until recently meant a pilgrimage to a deli. The French name Connétable deserves to be spoken in hushed, reverent tones – everything from the design of the can to the nurtured fish within. So a handful of these are a staple of my store cupboard, very good on toast as well with some slivers of gherkin or cucumber.

SERVES 3

2 x 115g	cans sardines
1	teaspoon grainy mustard
2	tablespoons finely chopped flat-leaf parsley, plus extra to serve
1	tablespoon extra virgin olive oil
2	teaspoons cider vinegar

Drain the sardines of oil and coarsely mash them in a medium bowl. Add all the remaining ingredients and continue to mash to a textured pâté. Transfer to a shallow serving bowl and scatter over a little more parsley. Cover and chill until required. It should keep well for up to a day.

ENERGY KCAL	CARBOHYDRATE G	SUGARS G	PROTEIN G	FAT G	SATURATED FAT G	SALT G
214	0.4	0.3	18.3	15.4	3.2	1.0

Tuna Niçoise

This quasi-salad is a multi-tasker – from mid-morning light grazing, to spooned over roast veg, or in neat boats of little lettuce leaves. Add cooked green beans, boiled eggs and anchovies for the full Niçoise treatment, and aim for sweet, ripe tomatoes, delicious olives and tuna (French and Spanish are particularly good) and a dash of your favourite olive oil.

SERVES 6

2 x 120g	cans 'no drain' tuna
2	tablespoons extra virgin olive oil
2	tablespoons lemon juice
	sea salt, black pepper
1	teaspoon finely chopped medium-hot red chilli
100g	pitted green and black olives, halved
150g	cherry tomatoes, halved or quartered
2	large handfuls of coarsely chopped flat-leaf parsley

Coarsely flake the tuna into a large bowl, and gently dress with the olive oil, lemon juice and a little seasoning. Mix in the chilli, olives, tomatoes and parsley. Cover and chill until required. Best on the day, but perfectly acceptable the day after too.

ENERGY KCAL	CARBOHYDRATE G	SUGARS G	PROTEIN G	FAT G	SATURATED FAT G	SALT G
110	1.1	1.1	10.5	6.6	1.0	0.9

Crab Tartare

The Bentley coupé of dips, this indulgence is guaranteed to illuminate an otherwise dull day. In the absence of a bowl of chips, some roasted or grilled courgette is hard to beat with this.

SERVES 2

100g	brown and white crabmeat (e.g. 50:50)
1	heaped teaspoon soured cream
1	heaped teaspoon mayonnaise
2	teaspoons small (non-pareil) capers, plus a few extra to serve
1	tablespoon finely chopped flat-leaf parsley, plus extra to serve
	cayenne pepper

Blend the crabmeat, soured cream and mayonnaise together in a small bowl. Stir in the capers, plus the parsley. Spread over the base of a small shallow dish, scatter over a little more parsley and a few capers and dust with cayenne pepper. Cover and chill for up to a day.

ENERGY KCAL	CARBOHYDRATE G	SUGARS G	PROTEIN G	FAT G	SATURATED FAT G	SALT G
128	0.5	0.4	10.2	9.5	1.8	0.8

Hot-smoked Salmon and Hazelnut Rillettes

Salmon with hazelnuts makes for a delightfully zany marriage. This is another chunky little number that sits on the right side of the tracks, and won't let you down if it happens to be a special occasion.

SERVES 4

150g	hot-smoked salmon fillets
2	teaspoons finely chopped shallot
50g	low-fat fromage frais
2	teaspoons extra virgin olive oil, plus extra to serve
1	teaspoon lemon juice, plus extra to serve
	sea salt, black pepper
1	tablespoon finely chopped flat-leaf parsley, plus extra to serve
1	tablespoon roast and chopped hazelnuts

Coarsely mash the salmon in a medium bowl, then add the shallot, the fromage frais, oil, lemon juice and a little seasoning and stir to blend. Mix in the parsley and two-thirds of the nuts and pile into a small shallow dish. Scatter over the remaining nuts, and drizzle over a little more oil and a squeeze of lemon juice, then finish with a sprinkling of parsley.

Cover and chill until required. It should keep well for up to a day.

ENERGY KCAL	CARBOHYDRATE G	SUGARS G	PROTEIN G	FAT G	SATURATED FAT G	SALT G
120	1.4	1.3	11.0	7.7	1.2	0.8

Salmon and Celery Mayonnaise

Flash-roasting a chunky fillet of salmon in this way is every bit as good as when it is poached for serving cold with mayonnaise. And this mélange has that quintessential wedding breakfast charm, less the rice salad, which we can live without (though a hunk of Rosemary Fake-accia, see page 27, is rather good). Salmon also tops the bill for eating cold, at least that is my own excuse for so frequently ensuring there are a couple of cooked fillets in the fridge.

SERVES 6

	groundnut oil, for greasing
500g	salmon fillet (skin on)
50g	mayonnaise
50g	0%-fat Greek yogurt
2	teaspoons cider vinegar, plus 1 teaspoon
	sea salt, black pepper
	inner section of 1 celery heart, trimmed and finely sliced
2	spring onions, trimmed, thinly sliced and chopped
1	tablespoon small (non-pareil) capers, rinsed
4	tablespoons finely chopped flat-leaf parsley, plus extra to serve

Preheat the oven to 220°C fan/240°C electric/gas mark 9 with a roasting pan big enough to hold the salmon inside. When it is very hot, trickle a little oil over the base of the dish, place the salmon, skin-side down in the dish, and roast for 15 minutes. Lift the fish onto a plate, discarding the skin, and press down with a spatula to coarsely flake it. Leave to cool for 10–15 minutes.

Meanwhile, blend the mayonnaise, yogurt, vinegar and some seasoning in a large bowl. Stir in the celery heart, spring onions, capers and parsley and then gently mix in the salmon, discarding any juices given out. Transfer to a serving bowl, or small shallow bowls. Scatter over a little more parsley, then cover and chill. It will be good for a couple of days.

ENERGY KCAL	CARBOHYDRATE G	SUGARS G	PROTEIN G	FAT G	SATURATED FAT G	SALT G
247	0.8	0.7	18.1	18.8	2.8	0.2

Pinchos and Nibbles

Time takes no prisoners, so with speed at its heart, pretty much the last thing this book is concerned with are drinks parties. But, here we are about to sashay into the world of eats of the kind that would be most at home with a glass of something in hand, and if you are anything like me who, at least inwardly, raises an eyebrow at being offered yet another starchy croûton or bowl of crisps, then you may find some relief in the suggestions that follow. And the notion that these are, in fact, to graze on throughout the day (convenient, fast and fresh), can only be an improvement to those other hand-me-rounds, the packet of choc chip cookies or bag of Haribos. These are the gaps they just might fill, particularly if you happen to be at home, although many are lunchbox-friendly too.

Pinchos is a great name for anything that you might take from plate to mouth in miniature, not as the name suggests 'pinched' between thumb and forefinger, but spiked with a skewer. Their remit is that of tapas, appetisers or nibbles, call these social eats what you will. Button mushrooms filled with melting scamorza, radishes piled with egg mayonnaise, chocolate walnuts with a touch of salt, or a spicy homemade mix of nuts and seeds. These are the sort of eats that I wish I could buy, but for the most part their simplicity and freshness puts paid to that. As their ingredient list will testify, they are all exceptionally basic, the most complex only runs to a wrap, here with a fine omelette standing in for the bread.

Parmesan Peppers

Worth making alone for the pleasure of filling the kitchen with the buttery scent of Parmesan toasting. These are sweet and juicy, the peppers left on the crisp side. Lovely for grazing on throughout the day, you could serve them as an aside to something sizzling, such as chicken or steak fresh from the grill. By way of character, they are readily padded out with olives, caper berries and Parma ham, that don't require any preparation.

SERVES 4

250g	mixed baby peppers*, stalks trimmed
200g	cherry tomatoes, halved downwards and thinly sliced across
	sea salt, black pepper
1	tablespoon extra virgin olive oil
50g	freshly grated Parmesan

Preheat the oven to 200°C fan/220°C electric/gas mark 7. Halve the peppers through the stalk, remove any seeds inside, and trim any membranes so you have a cavity to fill. Arrange these spaced slightly apart in a roasting pan.

Place the tomatoes in a medium bowl, season and add the olive oil, then toss. Fill the peppers with the tomatoes and juices, then scatter over the Parmesan – any that falls between the peppers will turn deliciously crisp. Bake for 20 minutes until golden. Lovely hot or cold.

Not too 'baby', about 8–10cm long so there is enough of a cavity to fill.

ENERGY KCAL	CARBOHYDRATE G	SUGARS G	PROTEIN G	FAT G	SATURATED FAT G	SALT G
113	4.9	4.7	5.6	7.3	2.9	0.2

Scamorza Mushrooms

Scamorza is an Italian cheese that has taken my house by storm. Uncooked it is no great shakes, firm to the point of rubbery, but it melts like a dream. In Italy it comes grilled like steak, which, eaten in the company of spinach laced with garlic and nutmeg, is about as good as lunch gets. In any case, these bijoux little mushrooms offer a small taste of what it can offer.

SERVES 4

2	tablespoons extra virgin olive oil
200g	button mushrooms, stalks removed*
	sea salt, black pepper
1	tablespoon finely chopped chives
approx. 50g	scamorza, cut into 1cm dice

Spread a tablespoon of oil over the base of a medium roasting pan, place in the oven and preheat it to 180°C fan/200°C electric/gas mark 6.

Arrange the mushrooms in the hot roasting pan spaced a little way apart, season, then drop a pinch of chives into each one and a square of cheese. Drizzle over the remaining oil and roast for 20 minutes until golden, then serve.

*Ideally, button mushroom stalks should pop out with a wiggle from side to side. If the stalks have been trimmed level with the cup, this is more fiddly.

ENERGY KCAL	CARBOHYDRATE G	SUGARS G	PROTEIN G	FAT G	SATURATED FAT G	SALT G
102	0.6	0.2	4.5	9.0	2.3	0.2

Smoked Salmon and Quail Egg Pinchos

A genuine pincho and the easiest of eats. If you want to cook your own eggs, then 2½ minutes simmering will leave them slightly wet in the centre, or 3 minutes if you prefer them hard-boiled. But ready cooked and shelled takes care of the fiddly bit.

MAKES 12/SERVES 4

12	strips of smoked salmon (approx. 3 x 8cm slices, or 100g, each cut across the grain)
12	cooked and peeled quail eggs
	black pepper

Sauce

50g	mayonnaise
50g	fromage frais or soured cream
	finely grated zest of 1 lemon, plus a squeeze of juice

For the skewers, pleat a strip of smoked salmon onto a cocktail stick concertina-style then pop a quail egg onto the end, thick-end first through to the middle. Combine all the ingredients for the sauce in a small bowl. (Both skewers and sauce can be prepared well in advance, in which case cover and chill.) Grind a little black pepper over the skewers to serve.

ENERGY KCAL	CARBOHYDRATE G	SUGARS G	PROTEIN G	FAT G	SATURATED FAT G	SALT G
209	0.9	0.8	10.0	18.3	4.0	0.8

Cheese and Chilli Crispies

These cheese crispies pay lip service to the all-time great among cheese eats, Roka Cheese Crispies, still available but without the tin that was so handy for knick-knacks. You want a good mature cheese here to max the flavour, but you can play around with Swiss-style cheeses like Gruyère, Comté and Abondance. Most of the oil is shed in the process of baking and then mopped up at the end, so they are not as high in fat as the cheese itself. But a couple of these is probably enough to ward off pre-dinner hunger with a drink, and some olives.

MAKES APPROX. 14–15/SERVES 7

150g	finely grated mature Gouda
2	heaped teaspoons finely chopped medium-hot red chilli

Preheat the oven to 160°C fan/180°C electric/gas mark 4, and line two baking sheets with baking paper. Drop heaped tablespoons of the cheese in mounds on the sheets, spaced well apart, then evenly scatter a little chopped chilli over each pile. Bake for 15–17 minutes until lacy and a very pale gold.

Leave to cool, then gently transfer, using a spatula or palette knife, to a double thickness of kitchen paper to drain, and pat the top with more paper. They are best served at room temperature, fresh on the day while they are crisp.

ENERGY KCAL	CARBOHYDRATE G	SUGARS G	PROTEIN G	FAT G	SATURATED FAT G	SALT G
41	2.0	1.6	3.5	2.1	1.3	0.4

Cucumber Canapés

Of all the options for replacing carby croûtons or a pastry base for canapés, these lightly pickled cucumber slices are my personal favourite. They're lovely with egg or crab mayonnaise, smoked salmon and soured cream, a few flakes of smoked mackerel, and many of the dips that feature in 'Dipping and Dolloping' (see pages 32–49).

MAKES APPROX. 30/SERVES 6

1	cucumber, ends discarded and sliced approx. 0.75cm thick
	sea salt
100ml	white wine vinegar or cider vinegar
125g	young goat's cheese
120–150g	cooked cold-water prawns
	finely chopped flat-leaf parsley or chopped chives

Season the cucumber slices with salt in a large bowl and set aside for 15 minutes. Then fill the bowl with cold water and give the cucumber a good sloosh before draining into a colander. Return it to the bowl. Bring 100ml of water and the vinegar to the boil in a small saucepan, pour over the cucumber and press to submerge the slices. Leave to cool for about 15 minutes, then drain into a colander and dry between a double thickness of kitchen paper.

Spread the cucumber slices with a little goat's cheese, place a couple of prawns on top and scatter with parsley or chives. (These can be made several hours in advance, in which case cover and chill.)

ENERGY KCAL	CARBOHYDRATE G	SUGARS G	PROTEIN G	FAT G	SATURATED FAT G	SALT G
66	1.9	1.9	7.1	3.1	1.6	0.4

Devilled Egg Radishes

Devilled eggs are something that I would love to love, were it only acceptable to eat the spicy egg mayonnaise in the middle and to leave the white. So in my eyes these are infinitely superior where a radish takes its place.

SERVES 6

4	medium eggs
150g	medium–large radishes, stalks and roots trimmed
25g	mayonnaise
1	teaspoon Dijon mustard
1	teaspoon cider vinegar or white wine vinegar
	sea salt, black pepper
3–4	salted anchovies, thickly sliced diagonally
	finely chopped chives

Bring a small pan of water to the boil, gently lower in the eggs and cook over a low heat for 10 minutes. Drain the water from the pan, refill with cold water and leave the eggs to cool for about 10 minutes.

Meanwhile, cut a thin slice off either side of each radish, and halve them through the stalk and root to give you two thick slices that will sit flat on a plate.

Shell the eggs, and discard two of the whites. Finely mash the remaining eggs and yolks in a medium bowl using a fork, then add the mayonnaise, mustard, vinegar and a little seasoning and combine. Mound a teaspoon of this onto each radish half and arrange on a plate. Place a sliver of anchovy in the middle of each one, scatter over some chives and serve.

ENERGY KCAL	CARBOHYDRATE G	SUGARS G	PROTEIN G	FAT G	SATURATED FAT G	SALT G
86	0.6	0.6	5.5	6.8	1.3	0.4

Spicy Nut and Seaweed Mix

Macadamias have such a fab buttery quality, it is surprising that we don't see more of them in cocktail nut form. These have the slightly abrasive coating that some of us guiltily crave in spicy peanuts, the ingredient list of which it is best not to consider. Here we have the integrity of real ingredients with the same hit. This is a stock recipe for any combination of nuts you might wish to dream up. I frequently find that I have a drawer full of half-used packets.

The only issue with tasty roast nuts is that it is all too easy to start snacking on them throughout the day. They are a great food to add into a low carb line-up, but a couple of handfuls a week, or just a few on a daily basis, is about right. Treat them as a treat.

MAKES 300G/SERVES 10

1	teaspoon unsalted butter, softened
150g	macadamia nuts
75g	pecan nuts
50g	pistachio nuts
25g	pumpkin seeds
1	tablespoon dark soy sauce (e.g. Kikkoman)
1	rounded teaspoon ground cumin
½–1	level teaspoon cayenne pepper
5g	nori or crispy seaweed thins (optional)

Preheat the oven to 160°C fan/180°C electric/gas mark 4. Smear the butter over the base of a roasting pan, then scatter the nuts and seeds in a thin layer on top. Roast for 15 minutes or until a pale gold, stirring halfway through.

Meanwhile, blend the soy sauce with the spices – ½ teaspoon of cayenne will be warming while 1 level teaspoon will give a definite bite.

Drizzle this over the nuts, stir them thoroughly until very lightly coated in the spice mix and return to the oven for about 5 minutes until toasty, golden and dried out. Give them a stir and leave to cool. If including the seaweed, crumble it over the cool nuts and store them in an airtight container. (They will keep well for ages.)

ENERGY KCAL	CARBOHYDRATE G	SUGARS G	PROTEIN G	FAT G	SATURATED FAT G	SALT G
220	2.2	1.5	4.0	21.2	2.9	0.3

BLTs

These tender lettuce boats provide a hit of that magical combination of bacon, lettuce, tomatoes and mayo. It's a slightly inexact art, as lettuce hearts come in different sizes, and it is easier to prize the leaves apart on some rather than others. So buy in a couple of packs and take it from there; any rejects can be sliced and added to a salad thereafter.

SERVES 4

100g	smoked streaky bacon, diced
2–3	large Little Gem hearts (or 4 small)
30g	mayonnaise
1	level teaspoon Dijon mustard
75g	cherry tomatoes, thinly sliced
	finely chopped flat-leaf parsley

Scatter the bacon over the base of a large, non-stick frying pan, separating out the pieces, and fry over a very low heat until the fat begins to render. Increase the heat to medium and cook for a further 5–7 minutes, stirring frequently, until the bacon is golden and crisp. Drain on a double thickness of kitchen paper.

Meanwhile, cut the base off the lettuce hearts, discard any damaged outer leaves and then separate the remainder. You want 12 little boats, 8–12 cm in length. You need 125g of lettuce for the filling: finely slice the remaining hearts, you can also use the slightly bigger undamaged leaves to make up the amount, if necessary. Combine the mayonnaise and mustard in a medium bowl, add the sliced lettuce, separating out the strands, and toss to coat it.

Fill the lettuce leaves with a little of the dressed lettuce. Scatter some tomatoes on top, then some crispy bacon and sprinkle with a little parsley.

ENERGY KCAL	CARBOHYDRATE G	SUGARS G	PROTEIN G	FAT G	SATURATED FAT G	SALT G
139	2.1	2.1	4.8	12.0	2.6	0.8

Mini Quiches

Mini quiches in muffin form. Lined with Parma ham on the outside that turns deliciously crispy, the filling is laced with mustard and Parmesan. They make great picnic and lunch box material, as well as a light lunch with the ever-appropriate green salad.

MAKES APPROX. 9

9	slices Parma ham*
2	medium eggs, plus 2 yolks
100g	quark
1	level teaspoon grainy mustard
1	level teaspoon Dijon mustard
50g	soya flour
½	teaspoon baking powder
50ml	whole milk
50g	freshly grated Parmesan
50g	cherry tomatoes, thinly sliced

Preheat the oven to 180°C fan/200°C electric/gas mark 6. Line 9 muffin holes within a 12-hole muffin tray with a slice of Parma ham, pleating it where necessary. Whisk together the eggs and yolks with the quark and mustards in a large bowl. Sift and add the flour and baking powder and whisk until smooth, then whisk in the milk and fold in 40g of the Parmesan. Fill the moulds by two-thirds, then scatter over the cherry tomatoes and the reserved Parmesan.

Bake for 17–20 minutes until lightly golden and risen. Leave to cool in the tray, when they will contract a little, then remove and serve. (These are at their best eaten on the day they are made, but still good the following day.)

*The ham should be thin without being so transparently fine that it tears easily.

ENERGY KCAL	CARBOHYDRATE G	SUGARS G	PROTEIN G	FAT G	SATURATED FAT G	SALT G
117	2.3	1.6	11.2	6.7	2.5	0.9

Egg Wraps

With these filled wraps, thin omelettes stand in for the tortilla. They are pretty as a picture sliced across; ideal for lunchboxes but equally a good hand-me-round at a party. Or, serve them sliced and arranged on a plate with a small dressed salad to the side.

MAKES 4

5	medium eggs
1	tablespoon extra virgin olive oil
	sea salt, black pepper

Whisk all the ingredients together with 1 tablespoon of water in a medium bowl. Fry the mixture a quarter at a time in a 24cm non-stick frying pan over a medium heat, as though making pancakes: cook each omelette for about 1 minute or until dry on the surface and golden beneath, then turn using a spatula and cook for a further 30–45 seconds. Stack them on a plate and leave to cool.

Continue with Serrano Ham and Goat's Cheese filling (below), or Smoked Salmon and Watercress (see page 64).

FOR NUTRITIONAL INFO SEE BELOW AND PAGE 64

Serrano Ham and Goat's Cheese Wraps

SERVES 4

1	red pepper, core and seeds removed, and cut into long thin strips
4	egg wraps (see above)
120g	fresh goat's cheese
8	basil leaves
8	slices Serrano ham, fat cut off
4	handfuls of baby spinach leaves
2	spring onions, trimmed and very finely chopped
1	cucumber, peeled, halved lengthways and deseeded, and cut into long batons about 1cm diameter

Trim the red pepper strips so they lie straight.

Lay the wraps out on a board and thinly spread with the goat's cheese. Lay the basil leaves on top, then the ham. Scatter over a single layer of spinach, then scatter over the spring onions.

Place the pepper and cucumber batons in a line about a quarter or a third of the way across each wrap, and then roll the wraps up tightly into a cylinder to enclose the filling. (Cover and chill for up to 24 hours until required.)

Slice the wraps into 2–3cm lengths using a small serrated knife, trimming and discarding the ragged ends. Lay the slices cut-side up on a plate and serve.

ENERGY KCAL	CARBOHYDRATE G	SUGARS G	PROTEIN G	FAT G	SATURATED FAT G	SALT G
244	4.3	4.2	19.1	16.2	5.3	1.5

Smoked Salmon and Watercress Wraps

SERVES 4

1	avocado, stoned, quartered, peeled and cut into long thin strips
	juice of ½ lemon
4	egg wraps (see page 62)
100g	cream cheese
200g	smoked salmon, brown meat cut out
	black pepper
4	handfuls of watercress or mustard and cress
2	tablespoons finely chopped chives
1	cucumber, peeled, halved lengthways and deseeded, and cut into batons about 1cm diameter

Toss the avocado with the lemon juice, then assemble the wraps as on page 62. Spread them with cream cheese, top with the salmon seasoned with black pepper, then the watercress and chives, and use the cucumber and avocado as the core.

ENERGY KCAL	CARBOHYDRATE G	SUGARS G	PROTEIN G	FAT G	SATURATED FAT G	SALT G
345	2.8	2.8	25.2	25.2	6.9	2.0

Parma Ham and Watermelon Appetisers

A classic, and timelessly elegant, a plate of these can be handed round for eating with fingers while you're waiting for the barbie to do its stuff. We tend to go for green-fleshed melons such as Cantaloupe or Honeydew, but watermelon makes a delicious variant, with a drizzle of honey to boost its sweetness and offset the ham.

SERVES 4

8   thin crescents of watermelon, rind cut off

8   slices Parma or other air-dried ham (e.g. Serrano)

1   teaspoon runny honey

coarsely chopped flat-leaf parsley, to serve

Cut out the inner section of melon with the seeds, which will leave you with a sickle shape. Wind a slice of ham around each watermelon segment and arrange on a serving dish. Drizzle over a thread of honey and scatter with parsley. (If making this in advance, arrange the melon and the Parma ham separately on a plate, then drizzle over the honey and scatter with parsley just before serving.)

ENERGY KCAL	CARBOHYDRATE G	SUGARS G	PROTEIN G	FAT G	SATURATED FAT G	SALT G
103	10.0	10.0	7.4	3.6	1.2	1.3

Sea Salt Choco Walnuts

Chocolate this dark, with just a fraction of sugar, spans the divide between sweet and savoury. With just the lightest coating on some nuts and a smattering of salt, these nibbles are quite at home with a drink, or at any other time of the day, and still offer the sensation of eating chocolate. They might just take the edge off that craving.

SERVES 4

100g	walnut halves
60g	dark chocolate (approx. 90% cocoa), broken into pieces
	Maldon sea salt, finely scrunched

Preheat the oven to 160°C fan/180°C electric/gas mark 4. Spread the walnut halves over the base of a roasting pan and roast for 10 minutes.

Meanwhile, gently melt the chocolate in a large, heatproof bowl set over a small saucepan of barely simmering water. Add the hot nuts and stir thoroughly to coat them, then spread these out on a sheet of baking paper on a small tray or plate, and lightly season with salt. Pop into the freezer for 15 minutes to set. Store in an airtight box in the fridge. (They will be good for several days.)

ENERGY KCAL	CARBOHYDRATE G	SUGARS G	PROTEIN G	FAT G	SATURATED FAT G	SALT G
276	4.4	2.7	5.8	25.4	6.7	0.5

Soups, Stews and Smoothies

Smoothies are a potential minefield for those avoiding sugar. Many is the innocent and alluring creamy glass of milkshake-esque delight that contains a small basket of fruit, and while sugars that are integral to a whole fruit are considered to be nutritious, they count as 'free sugars' when they are part of a smoothie. These are sugars deemed to be gratuitous, along with added sugars, and ones that we should limit. In any event, while it is easy to get carried away eating lots of fruit in the belief it is healthy – which it is – two pieces a day is more than enough, and even then there is a steep sliding scale, with berries containing the least number of carbs, and bananas, cherries and grapes the most. So a carefully considered cocktail, together with creamy ingredients that are low in fat and high in protein, and the odd vegetable that marries discreetly with the fruit, is the way to go. I am also a great believer in watering smoothies down, so they are thirst-quenching as well as nurturing.

Soups, on the other hand, are every low carber's best friend, a natural that lends itself to any number of vegetables. Courgettes, leafy greens, cauliflower, celeriac and leeks are just some that make fab soups but, unlike potato, squash and beetroot, they have a low carbohydrate content. But a word of caution on the stock front, I would avoid powders, if possible, which rarely make a natural read on the ingredient front, as well as being loaded with salt. Fresh stocks are the ideal.

While baguette might be off the menu, there are still all manner of ways of pairing soups with little asides that marry with their character, so for instance, a little smoked salmon and crisp radish salad with an avocado soup, or a young goat's cheese with some small lettuce leaves and spring onions to go with a cauliflower soup. There are endless ideas for spinning them out.

Mango and Coconut Smoothie

Silken tofu is a world apart from the standard bean curd, which tends to foster a love-hate relationship and is a rough diamond by comparison. Fresh silken tofu is tender, soft as butter and as good eaten with a shake of soy sauce and a squeeze of lime juice as it is included in sweet dishes. It could be this involves a visit to a deli that stocks it, but it's worth the trip.

SERVES 1

100g	mango flesh
100g	fresh silken tofu
1	heaped teaspoon coconut yogurt
1	tablespoon lime juice
1	teaspoon granulated stevia (i.e. equivalent to 1 teaspoon sugar)
	seeds of ½ passionfruit

Whizz all the ingredients, except the passionfruit seeds, with 85ml of water in a blender until smooth. Pour into a 300ml highball glass and spoon over the passionfruit seeds before drinking.

ENERGY KCAL	CARBOHYDRATE G	SUGARS G	PROTEIN G	FAT G	SATURATED FAT G	SALT G
162	17.5	15.4	6.1	6.1	3.3	trace

Kiwi and Cucumber Smoothie

I love the clean profile of this smoothie; it's snappy and sharp, and the raspberry quark float lets it down gently and provides a decadent touch. It's hard to have too many of these berries, you can scatter a few over the top too. Cucumber is a great ingredient to include in smoothies; it offers body and goodness without the calories or sugar, and it marries with any number of fruits. Think of it as melon without the carbs.

SERVES 1

2	kiwi fruit, peeled and coarsely chopped
150g	cucumber, peeled and coarsely chopped
	juice of ½ lime
	granulated stevia (optional)
30g	raspberries
1	rounded tablespoon quark

Whizz the kiwi fruit, cucumber and lime juice in a blender until smooth. I like a sharp edge, but you could add a little stevia to taste, if wished. Mash the raspberries with the quark in a small bowl; again a little stevia can be added to taste. Pour the smoothie into a 300ml highball glass and drop the raspberry quark in the centre, then dive in with a teaspoon.

ENERGY KCAL	CARBOHYDRATE G	SUGARS G	PROTEIN G	FAT G	SATURATED FAT G	SALT G
141	18.2	17.8	7.7	1.6	0.0	0.1

Herb Lassi

A lassi is a drink for a summer's morning or a scorching day, sipped once the heat has settled in. This has lots of herbs, a little spice and is spiked with shavings of ice.

SERVES 2

	handful each of flat-leaf parsley leaves, chopped chives, basil leaves
1	teaspoon caster sugar (or equivalent of granulated stevia)
400g	full-fat natural yogurt
200g	ice cubes
	sea salt
	ground cumin, for dusting

If your blender has an ice-crushing function (e.g. Magimix), put everything in the jug and liquidise to a slush. Failing this, before blending, put the ice cubes in two plastic bags, one inside the other, seal and coarsely crush using a rolling pin. Divide the lassi between two 300ml highball glasses and dust with cumin. Serve with straws.

ENERGY KCAL	CARBOHYDRATE G	SUGARS G	PROTEIN G	FAT G	SATURATED FAT G	SALT G
170	15.9	15.7	11.9	6.3	3.8	0.4

Cucumber, Watermelon and Mint Soup

This plays to the charm of a gazpacho, an artful balance of sweet and sour, courtesy of the watermelon and a little cider vinegar, with a plentiful addition of herbs that give it a lively edge.

SERVES 4

2	handfuls of mint leaves, plus a few to garnish
2	cucumbers, ends trimmed, peeled and coarsely chopped
300g	watermelon flesh, deseeded and coarsely chopped
1	tablespoon cider vinegar
1	small or ½ garlic clove, peeled and chopped
3	spring onions, trimmed and coarsely chopped
3	tablespoons extra virgin olive oil
	sea salt
	ice cubes, to serve

Whizz all the ingredients together in a blender, in batches, if necessary. Pass through a sieve into a large bowl, then taste for seasoning.

Ladle the cold* soup into small bowls or cups. Pop a few ice cubes into the centre of each bowl and a few tiny mint leaves. The soup can be covered and chilled for up to a day.

A tip for ready-chilled soup is to store your cucumbers and watermelon in the fridge.

ENERGY KCAL	CARBOHYDRATE G	SUGARS G	PROTEIN G	FAT G	SATURATED FAT G	SALT G
150	8.4	8.1	2.9	11.1	1.4	trace

Green Goddess Soup

This super-healthy raw vegetable soup is easily glam enough for a summer lunch or barbecue. It also lends itself to a spoon of crabmeat, a few cooked prawns or slivers of smoked salmon in its midst, either as well as or instead of the courgette.

SERVES 4

2	cucumbers, ends removed, and cut into pieces
2	sticks of celery heart (without leaves), thickly sliced
1	green pepper, core and seeds discarded, coarsely chopped
	flesh of 2 large avocados
1	small garlic clove, peeled and coarsely chopped
1	spring onion, trimmed and thickly sliced
1	teaspoon finely chopped medium-hot green chilli
	handful of basil leaves
75ml	extra virgin olive oil, plus 1 tablespoon for the courgette
1	generous tablespoon sherry vinegar
2	rounded teaspoons caster sugar
	sea salt

TO SERVE

100g	fine spiralised courgette
	squeeze of lemon juice
	coarsely chopped flat-leaf parsley

Whizz all the ingredients for the soup together in a blender, then taste and adjust the seasoning, if necessary. Pour into a bowl, cover and chill until required. The soup will keep overnight.

To serve, toss the courgette with a tablespoon of olive oil, the lemon juice and a little salt. Serve a pile in the middle of each bowl of soup, scattered with parsley.

ENERGY KCAL	CARBOHYDRATE G	SUGARS G	PROTEIN G	FAT G	SATURATED FAT G	SALT G
369	7.3	7.0	4.8	34.1	5.2	0.1

Chilled Avocado Soup

A soup that illustrates in the same way as the Kiwi and Cucumber Smoothie (see page 70) just what a good friend cucumber can be – it readily adopts the role of stock in a cold or chilled soup. This silky pale-green bowlful has the edge over many avocado soups that need to be slurped as soon as they are made, as it will be good for half a day plus. Instead of that hunk of bread, a little smoked salmon and radish salad on the side goes down a treat (see below).

SERVES 4

2	avocados, halved and stoned
3	cucumbers, ends discarded, peeled and cut into pieces
2	shallots, peeled and coarsely chopped
1	tablespoon cider vinegar
3	tablespoons extra virgin olive oil, plus extra to serve
	shake of Tabasco
	sea salt, black pepper
	TO SERVE
	ice cubes
	slivers of spring onion

Scoop the avocado flesh into a blender, add all the remaining ingredients and blend until smooth. Serve with a drizzle of oil, a couple of ice cubes and some slivers of spring onion. The soup can be covered and chilled, and ideally eaten on the day it is made, but it is good for a few hours at least.

ENERGY KCAL	CARBOHYDRATE G	SUGARS G	PROTEIN G	FAT G	SATURATED FAT G	SALT G
223	0.8	0.8	1.5	23.1	4.2	trace

On the Side — Radish Salad and Smoked Salmon

150g	breakfast radishes, trimmed and thinly sliced
2	tablespoons mayonnaise
	sea salt
6	tablespoons alfalfa sprouts
	black pepper
125–150g	sliced smoked salmon, cut into wide strips
	lemon wedges, to serve

Mix the radishes with the mayonnaise in a bowl and season to taste with salt. Place a tablespoon of alfalfa sprouts on four plates, spreading them out a little. Spoon the radish salad on top, then scatter over a few more sprouts.

Grind some black pepper over the smoked salmon and serve alongside the radish salad with lemon wedges.

ENERGY KCAL	CARBOHYDRATE G	SUGARS G	PROTEIN G	FAT G	SATURATED FAT G	SALT G
123	1.1	1.1	8.6	9.3	1.2	1.1

Iced Tomato and Almond Soup

This fabulous orange-coloured gazpacho is a marriage between a traditional tomato one and an ajo blanco, *made using almonds. It benefits from being made an hour ahead and chilled, but you can help it along the way by chilling the tomatoes first.*

SERVES 4

1kg	orange cherry tomatoes, plus a couple, finely sliced, to serve
1	garlic clove, peeled and chopped
1	heaped teaspoon chopped medium-hot red chilli
2	heaped teaspoons chopped onion
50ml	extra virgin olive oil, plus extra to serve
½	tablespoon red wine vinegar or sherry vinegar
1	rounded teaspoon caster sugar
2	rounded teaspoons Maldon sea salt
75g	ground almonds

TO SERVE

ice cubes

finely chopped chives

Put all the ingredients except the ground almonds in a blender and reduce to a purée, then pass through a sieve into a large bowl – you will need to do this in batches. Rinse out the blender and purée the soup again with the almonds.

Ladle into bowls and pop a few ice cubes into each one, drizzle with olive oil and scatter with a couple of sliced tomatoes and the chopped chives. The soup can be covered and chilled for at least a day.

ENERGY KCAL	CARBOHYDRATE G	SUGARS G	PROTEIN G	FAT G	SATURATED FAT G	SALT G
305	11.6	11.1	6.7	23.3	2.7	1.2

Miso Soup with Tofu

The best route to a good miso soup that sings with umami and provides a satisfying savoury hit, is a fresh unpasteurised miso. This comes in any number of different flavours made with various grains; we have a particular weakness for ones with chilli in this house. The chilled cabinet of a health food store is a good hunting ground, as is a Japanese deli or supermarket.

SERVES 4

400ml	light vegetable stock
50g	mangetout, topped and tailed, cut into long fine strips and halved
3	level tablespoons brown miso (e.g. barley or rice)
100g	fresh silken tofu, cut into 1–2cm dice

TO SERVE

2	thin spring onions, trimmed and finely sliced diagonally
	coarsely chopped coriander

Bring the stock to the boil in a small saucepan, add the mangetout and blanch for 1 minute. Blend a little of the stock with the miso to a smooth, thin paste in a medium bowl – if necessary give it a quick whisk – then stir this into the soup base.

Divide the tofu between four cupped bowls, ladle in the soup, and serve scattered with spring onions and coriander.

ENERGY KCAL	CARBOHYDRATE G	SUGARS G	PROTEIN G	FAT G	SATURATED FAT G	SALT G
53	5.7	2.9	3.5	1.5	0.2	1.7

Watercress and Pistachio Soup

Pistachio nuts give this soup a soothing homespun texture, thick and faintly mealy. Their scent after a quick spell in hot butter works a treat with the watercress, while the pomegranate challenges its slight bitterness. It is a soup that suggests that all is well with the world. You might like to crumble a little goat's cheese into the finished soup for added pleasure.

SERVES 6

1.1 litres	chicken or vegetable stock
50g	unsalted butter
50g	pistachio nuts, coarsely chopped, plus a few extra to serve
250g	watercress, leaves and fine stalks
300g	celeriac, peeled, cut into 5–7cm chunks and finely sliced
	sea salt, black pepper
2	tablespoons pomegranate syrup, to serve

Bring the stock to the boil in a small saucepan. Melt the butter in a large saucepan over a medium heat, add the nuts and fry for 30–60 seconds until nice and buttery, stirring constantly. Add the watercress and stir until it wilts. Add the celeriac and cook for a minute longer, stirring occasionally, then pour in the boiling stock and add some seasoning. Simmer the soup for 6 minutes, then whizz it in a blender, in batches, until smooth.

Gently reheat if necessary and serve in warm bowls with a thread (1 teaspoon) of pomegranate syrup and a few extra pistachios. It is also good chilled.

ENERGY KCAL	CARBOHYDRATE G	SUGARS G	PROTEIN G	FAT G	SATURATED FAT G	SALT G
185	11.2	9.9	4.2	12.3	5.1	1.4

Spinach and Spring Onion Soup

Spinach always makes for a daring green soup with a deliciously gloopy texture, and here a few peas add a mealy sweetness. For the full monty, make up some lettuce cups with hot-smoked salmon (see below).

SERVES 4

2	bunches of spring onions (approx. 200g total), trimmed and sliced
30g	unsalted butter
	sea salt, black pepper
500g	spinach
100g	shelled fresh or frozen peas
750ml	vegetable stock
	freshly grated nutmeg
4	heaped teaspoons soured cream, to serve

Finely chop a tablespoon of the spring onions and set aside. Melt the butter in a large saucepan over a lowish heat, add the remaining spring onions, season generously with salt and fry for about 5 minutes until softened and glossy, stirring occasionally. Add the spinach, cover and cook for 10 minutes until wilted, stirring halfway through. Add the peas and the stock, bring to the boil and simmer over a low heat for 5 minutes.

Whizz it, in batches, in a food processor until you have a good mealy-textured soup, adding a little black pepper and nutmeg to taste.

Gently reheat if necessary and serve the soup in warm bowls with a spoon of soured cream in the centre. Dust with extra nutmeg and scatter over the reserved spring onions.

ENERGY KCAL	CARBOHYDRATE G	SUGARS G	PROTEIN G	FAT G	SATURATED FAT G	SALT G
201	10.3	7.9	7.0	12.7	7.1	1.7

On the Side Lettuce Cups with Salmon and Capers

40g	soured cream
	squeeze of lemon juice
	black pepper
125g	hot-smoked salmon flakes
2	teaspoons small (non-pareil) capers, rinsed
8	Little Gem lettuce leaves, 8–10cm long (approx. 2 hearts)
	finely chopped flat-leaf parsley, to serve

Combine the soured cream, lemon juice and some black pepper in a medium bowl and fold in the salmon. Mix to a coarse paste, then fold in the capers. Drop a heaped teaspoon of this in the centre of each lettuce leaf and scatter with parsley.

ENERGY KCAL	CARBOHYDRATE G	SUGARS G	PROTEIN G	FAT G	SATURATED FAT G	SALT G
86	1.1	1.1	8.5	5.3	2.1	0.8

Leek and Mustard Soup

Like all the best leek soups this is pale green and silky, wholesome in a way that is unique to this vegetable. In truth, I know very few people who like leeks as they are, but soup is a different matter. Mustard makes a natural companion. Should you ever find yourself in the environs of a mustard shop such as one of the Maille boutiques, ensure you stop off and taste. My favourite find as I write is a chestnut Dijon, a better habit to acquire than their white truffle mustard. This soup would sit nicely with a few trimmed and halved radishes, and fine shavings of a mature Gouda or Mimolette.

SERVES 6

50g	unsalted butter
1	large onion, peeled and chopped
2	garlic cloves, peeled and finely chopped
900g	leeks (trimmed weight), sliced
150ml	white wine
1.2 litres	chicken or vegetable stock
	sea salt, black pepper
2	rounded teaspoons Dijon mustard
2	heaped tablespoons soured cream
	finely chopped dill, to serve

Melt the butter in a large saucepan over a medium-low heat and fry the onion for a few minutes until softened, stirring occasionally, then add the garlic and leeks and continue to fry for about 10 minutes until silky and soft, without colouring. Add the wine and reduce until syrupy, then add the stock and some seasoning, bring to the boil and simmer for 10 minutes.

Purée the soup in a blender, in batches, with the mustard; it should remain textured. Gently reheat if necessary and serve in warm bowls with a dollop of soured cream and a little dill scattered over.

ENERGY KCAL	CARBOHYDRATE G	SUGARS G	PROTEIN G	FAT G	SATURATED FAT G	SALT G
216	8.7	6.7	8.3	13.6	7.4	1.0

Cauliflower Soup with Za'atar

Few vegetables can put on a one-man show in the way cauliflower can. This speedy soup is a gem for the repertoire. Za'atar oil gives a lively finish, or add a generous dollop of coconut yogurt. You could serve this with young goat's cheese, baby lettuce leaves and spring onions.

SERVES 4

30g	unsalted butter
1	onion, peeled and chopped
1	small cauliflower, cut into small florets (approx. 600g)
100ml	white wine
	sea salt, black pepper
1	heaped teaspoon za'atar
3	tablespoons extra virgin olive oil
1	tablespoon lemon juice

Melt the butter in a large saucepan over a medium-low heat, add the onion, cauliflower and wine and cook for 10–15 minutes, stirring occasionally, until it changes from a chalky to a translucent white, without colouring. Add 700ml of water, plenty of salt and a little pepper, bring to the boil, cover and cook over a low heat for 15 minutes. Purée in a blender and return to the saucepan and reheat gently if necessary.

Combine the za'atar, oil and lemon juice in a small bowl and serve drizzled over each bowl of soup.

ENERGY KCAL	CARBOHYDRATE G	SUGARS G	PROTEIN G	FAT G	SATURATED FAT G	SALT G
216	7.5	4.8	4	16.2	5.4	trace

Minestrone Pronto

This simple minestrone centres on broccoli with lots of parsley. Any number of different pestos or chilled tubs of sauce will work. Serve with slivers of fig and finely shaved pecorino.

SERVES 4

approx. 4	tablespoons extra virgin olive oil
1	red onion, peeled and chopped
1	celery heart, trimmed and sliced
4	garlic cloves, peeled and finely chopped
400g	long-stem broccoli, sliced 1cm thick
900ml	vegetable stock
	sea salt, black pepper
2	handfuls of flat-leaf parsley, plus extra
120g	pesto

Heat 3 tablespoons of olive oil in a large saucepan over a medium heat and fry the onion and celery for about 10 minutes until softened and lightly coloured, stirring occasionally. Stir in the garlic and broccoli and fry for another couple of minutes. Add the stock and some seasoning, bring to the boil and simmer for 10 minutes.

Whizz half the soup in a food processor with the parsley to a textured purée, then return to the pan to gently reheat, stir in the pesto and taste for seasoning.

Serve in warm bowls with an extra drizzle of oil, scattered with a little parsley.

ENERGY KCAL	CARBOHYDRATE G	SUGARS G	PROTEIN G	FAT G	SATURATED FAT G	SALT G
308	10.7	7.4	5.2	26	3.9	2.2

Thai Curried Chicken Soup

This has all the charm of a Thai curry but succeeds in being lighter. Although the recipe list runs to a fair number of ingredients, it is super easy. You could also pad it out with some soya or edamame bean noodles. As you need a fair bit of cooked chicken, it is a good soup to make post-roast, and worth buying a bigger bird than you might want at the time. It also lends itself to cooked turkey. A little torn basil added at the end does not go amiss.

SERVES 6

2	tablespoons groundnut or vegetable oil
1	rounded teaspoon green curry paste
3	banana shallots, peeled and thinly sliced
400ml	chicken stock
400ml	light coconut milk
1½	tablespoons lime juice
1	level teaspoon palm or light muscovado sugar
1½	teaspoons Maldon sea salt
300g	cooked chicken, shredded
300g	beansprouts
1	teaspoon fish sauce (nam pla)
4	tablespoons coarsely chopped coriander, plus extra to serve
	finely sliced medium-hot green or red chilli, seeds discarded, to serve (optional)

Heat the oil in a medium saucepan over a medium-low heat, add the curry paste and stir it around, then add the shallots and cook for a few minutes until they start to soften and are coated with the paste. Pour in the stock and coconut milk, and add the lime juice, sugar and salt. Bring to the boil (you can turn the heat up for this), and simmer over a very low heat for 15 minutes, stirring frequently, until the soup is creamy.

Add the chicken and beansprouts, bring back to the boil and simmer for a couple of minutes longer. Stir in the fish sauce and coriander and serve in warm bowls scattered with extra coriander and, if wished, a slice or two of chilli.

ENERGY KCAL	CARBOHYDRATE G	SUGARS G	PROTEIN G	FAT G	SATURATED FAT G	SALT G
206	5.2	3.9	20.3	11.0	4.9	1.1

Leafy Green Soup with Lemon and Parmesan

The lemon and garlic spar with the lively bitterness of the spring greens. A strong case for a good homemade broth here, or a good fresh stock. Lovely showered with lots of Parmesan.

SERVES 4

2	tablespoons extra virgin olive oil
1	celery heart, trimmed and sliced
2	leeks, trimmed and sliced
3	garlic cloves, peeled and finely chopped
200g	baby spring greens, trimmed and thickly sliced
1 litre	chicken stock
1	tablespoon lemon juice, plus 2 strips of zest removed with a vegetable peeler
	sea salt, black pepper
4	heaped teaspoons freshly grated Parmesan

Heat the olive oil in a medium saucepan over a medium heat and fry the celery and leeks for about 5 minutes, until translucent and starting to soften, stirring frequently. Stir in the garlic and cook for a minute or two longer until just starting to colour. Add half the leaves and once these start to reduce, add the remainder and cook for a further 2–3 minutes until wilted. Add the stock, lemon zest and some seasoning, bring to the boil, cover and simmer over a low heat for 10 minutes. The soup can be prepared to this point well in advance.

To serve, reheat if necessary, discard the zest, stir in the lemon juice and taste for seasoning. Serve in warm bowls scattered with Parmesan.

ENERGY KCAL	CARBOHYDRATE G	SUGARS G	PROTEIN G	FAT G	SATURATED FAT G	SALT G
156	3.2	2.8	9.9	10.6	2.5	1.2

Herby Seafood Stew

The foundation of this stew cooks in less than 5 minutes, a speed that is mirrored by its freshness – it comes loaded with coriander and mint, and cucumber makes the most delicate of vegetables when lightly cooked. Like all the best fish stews, you can vary the seafood. The ideal is at least one meaty fish and something like prawns to offer a change in pace.

SERVES 4

2	tablespoons extra virgin olive oil
1	bunch of spring onions (approx. 10), trimmed and sliced 1cm thick
1	teaspoon finely chopped medium-hot green chilli
1	cucumber, peeled, halved lengthways and sliced the thickness of a £1 coin
250g	baby spinach
30g	mint leaves, coarsely chopped
30g	coriander leaves, coarsely chopped, plus a little extra to serve
300ml	fish stock
	sea salt, black pepper
400g	salmon fillets, skinned, cut into 3cm pieces
200g	cooked and peeled king prawns
1	tablespoon lime juice

Heat the oil in a large casserole over a medium heat. Add the spring onions and chilli and fry for about 1 minute, stirring frequently until glossy, then add the cucumber and fry for 1–2 minutes longer, stirring occasionally, until it starts to turn translucent. Add the spinach in two goes, stirring until this wilts, then stir in the herbs. Add the stock and some seasoning and bring to the boil, then stir the salmon into the soup, cover and cook for 4 minutes, gently folding in the prawns halfway through. Again, very gently, stir in the lime juice and check the seasoning. Serve in warm bowls with a little more coriander scattered over.

ENERGY KCAL	CARBOHYDRATE G	SUGARS G	PROTEIN G	FAT G	SATURATED FAT G	SALT G
364	3.5	2.5	33.6	23.3	3.9	1.2

Eggs and Fritters

Eggs have always been handy, but it is only now that they are emerging from under their bushel and into the light. Eggs are exceptional in being low in saturated fat but high in cholesterol. For years we were advised to restrict our consumption to just a few a week, in the belief they were associated with heart disease. But it is now known that moderate egg consumption does not contribute significantly to overall cholesterol and the risk of heart disease, as previously feared, so once again we can stop counting. It is also possible to buy eggs with an enriched omega-3 fatty acid profile achieved by manipulating the hen's feed. So eggs are a high-quality source of protein that has the advantage of being more affordable than most meat and fish sources, and the more styles of cooking them that we take on board the better.

Poached, fried, soft-boiled or scrambled eggs may be a given at breakfast or as a light supper, and Spanish tortillas and creamy French-style omelettes filled with wild mushrooms, leafy herbs and melting cheese are also a staple for many. But their talents go so much further, and you can capture the spirit of pretty much any culture in an omelette of some description, be it a spicy Indian omelette or a tender Japanese rolled omelette spiked with oyster sauce. And it is these jazzy flavour scenarios that have captured my imagination of late.

The potential for eggs being cooked in different ways is also greater than we tend to allow. I am the world's worst omelette cook if, that is, we are talking about a classic French-style folded omelette – the notion that 'anyone can cook an omelette' excludes me. So my quest when cooking eggs has always been for foolproof methods. Frittatas are a given, zero sleight of hand called for making eggs the Italian way, but I also love open omelettes, not dissimilar in technique, you simply make them thinner and pile them higher with tasty little additions of your choice in the way that you might a pizza, and they do a remarkably good job of standing in. And eggs make lovely fritters, with seasonal vegetables and herbs, something like a savoury pancake.

Pizza Omelettes

These pizza-style omelettes have taken my kitchen by storm, especially if I am eating alone or when there are just two of us. Like all the best pizzas they are more about the goodies on top than the base, here just a thin and delicate omelette that is golden underneath and tender and creamy in the middle. They take all of 5 minutes to cook, and will lend themselves to any mélange of cheese, olives, roast veg and cured meats, in true pizza style, and the fridge is likely to offer all manner of scenarios on this score.

Pizza Omelette with Mozzarella and Chorizo

SERVES 2

3	medium eggs
	sea salt, black pepper
1	teaspoon extra virgin olive oil
100g	cocktail or cherry tomatoes, thinly sliced
40g	chorizo sausage, thinly sliced
75g	mozzarella or scamorza*, cut into 1cm dice

Whisk the eggs with a little seasoning in a medium bowl, and have the remaining ingredients prepped and at the ready.

Preheat the grill, and also heat a 24cm non-stick frying pan with a heatproof handle over a medium heat for a few minutes. Drizzle the oil over the base of the pan, then tip in the eggs and swirl to coat the base. Cook for 1–2 minutes until puffy around the edges and golden underneath. At the same time, arrange the sliced tomatoes over the top of the omelette, then scatter over the chorizo and cheese. Pop under the grill for 2–3 minutes, or until golden and sizzling. Serve straight away, or while it is still warm.

*Scamorza is a smoked mozzarella-type cheese with a nice firm texture. It's particularly good grilled or toasted.

ENERGY KCAL	CARBOHYDRATE G	SUGARS G	PROTEIN G	FAT G	SATURATED FAT G	SALT G
321	2.2	2.0	22.9	26.1	10.1	1.4

Pizza Omelette with Artichokes and Pesto

SERVES 2

3	medium eggs
	sea salt, black pepper
	handful of rocket
approx. 1	tablespoon extra virgin olive oil
100g	anti-pasti artichoke hearts (e.g. Sacla), thinly sliced
1	tablespoon pesto, either classic basil or sun-dried tomato
25g	finely shaved Parmesan

Have all the ingredients prepped and at the ready. Whisk the eggs with a little seasoning in a small bowl. Put the rocket in a medium bowl and toss with a couple of teaspoons of oil to coat it.

Preheat the grill, and also heat a 24cm non-stick frying pan with a heatproof handle over a medium heat for a few minutes. Drizzle a teaspoon of oil over the base of the pan, then tip in the eggs and swirl to coat the base. Cook for 1–2 minutes until puffy around the edges and golden underneath, and at the same time scatter over the artichokes and the rocket, dot with the pesto and scatter over the cheese. Pop under the grill for 2–3 minutes or until golden and sizzling. Serve straight away, or while it is still warm.

ENERGY KCAL	CARBOHYDRATE G	SUGARS G	PROTEIN G	FAT G	SATURATED FAT G	SALT G
282	1.2	1.0	17.5	22.9	6.3	0.8

Pizza Omelette with Tomato and Gruyère

SERVES 2

100g	cherry tomatoes, quartered
3	spring onions, trimmed and thinly sliced
approx. 1	tablespoon extra virgin olive oil, plus a little extra for cooking
3	medium eggs
75g	coarsely grated Gruyère
	sea salt, black pepper

Have all the ingredients prepped and at the ready. Toss the tomatoes and spring onions in a small bowl with a tablespoon of oil and whisk the eggs with a little seasoning in another small bowl.

Heat the grill, and also a 24cm non-stick frying pan with a heatproof handle over a medium heat for a few minutes. Drizzle a teaspoon of oil over the base of the pan, then tip in the eggs and swirl to coat the base. Cook for 1–2 minutes until puffy around the edges and golden underneath, and at the same time scatter over the cheese, then the tomato and spring onion. Pop under the grill for 2–3 minutes or until golden and sizzling. Serve straight away, or while it is still warm.

ENERGY KCAL	CARBOHYDRATE G	SUGARS G	PROTEIN G	FAT G	SATURATED FAT G	SALT G
340	2.2	2.2	21.6	26.8	10.9	1.0

Japanese Omelette

For lovers of savoury breakfasts, travelling can be a lottery. Will it be Continental breads and fruit salad, or an all-you-can-eat cereal buffet (my idea of hell)? This has nothing to do with carbs, I simply favour savoury over sweet at the start of the day. My ideal hotel offering is more in line with thick slices of a young Spanish cheese with equally thick slices of large beefsteak tomatoes and some air-dried ham.

Japan would certainly prove an excellent place to find yourself, and this line-up of seared salmon, avocado and tender rolled omelette was inspired by just such a breakfast. It also makes a lovely supper with a pile of edamame bean noodles. This is laced with what we regard as healthy oils, in the eggs, the salmon and avocado; one of those dishes that is featherlight to eat but will gently sustain you throughout the day, or night, without feeling overly full.

SERVES 4

6	medium eggs
1	tablespoon light soy sauce
1	teaspoon sesame oil
1	avocado, halved and stoned
½	lemon
	cayenne pepper
200g	skinned salmon fillets, sliced into strips 8–10cm long and 1cm wide
3	spring onions, trimmed and thinly sliced
1	tablespoon toasted sesame seeds
1	tablespoon oyster sauce
1	tablespoon finely sliced nori or crisp seaweed thins

Whisk the eggs with the soy sauce and sesame oil in a medium bowl. Cut the avocado in its skin into long thin strips and scoop these out of the shell onto the side of four plates using a dessertspoon. Squeeze over some lemon juice and dust with cayenne pepper. Have all the other ingredients prepped and ready.

Heat a large, non-stick frying pan over a high heat for several minutes, and fry the salmon strips for about 1 minute on the first side until golden, and for 30 seconds on the second side; the fish should feel firm when pressed. Arrange these beside the avocado.

Turn the heat down to medium-high, tip in a quarter of the egg mixture and swirl to coat the base. Fry until it starts to dry out, leaving a thin film of wet egg on the surface, then fold it over several times like a pancake. Place this beside the salmon and avocado, and then cook a further three omelettes.

Scatter the spring onion and sesame seeds over the omelettes, then drizzle the oyster sauce over the salmon and scatter with the seaweed. Serve straight away.

ENERGY KCAL	CARBOHYDRATE G	SUGARS G	PROTEIN G	FAT G	SATURATED FAT G	SALT G
291	1.8	1.0	22.4	21.3	4.8	1.4

Dutch Boerenomelet

I thought frittatas were the easiest omelette possible until I discovered this brilliant Dutch omelette. Boerenomelet means 'farmer's omelette', which is a catch-all for any veggies you want to fry up and include, but always with some ham, melting Dutch cheese and lots of herbs. You simply cook one side, scatter all the bits and bobs over the top and then fold it over. The genuine thing usually contains potato, but it certainly isn't lacking without. A mixture of leeks and mushrooms is heavenly with the cheese and eggs.

SERVES 2

10g	unsalted butter
1	teaspoon extra virgin olive oil
1	leek, trimmed, halved lengthways and thinly sliced
75g	mushrooms (ideally wild), trimmed and torn or sliced
	sea salt, black pepper
4	medium eggs
3	tablespoons skimmed milk
1	heaped tablespoon finely chopped chives
1	heaped tablespoon finely chopped flat-leaf parsley, plus extra to serve
50g	grated mature Gouda
75g	roast ham, diced

Heat the butter and oil in a large, non-stick frying pan over a medium heat. Add the leek and mushrooms, season and fry for 5–7 minutes until softened and starting to colour, then remove to a small bowl. In the meantime, whisk the eggs with the milk and some seasoning in a medium bowl, then stir in the herbs.

Tip the egg mixture into the pan and briefly scramble with a fork until half-set. Cook for about 2 minutes, while scattering the cheese, ham and leek mixture over the top. The omelette should be nice and golden underneath. Fold it over using a spatula and slip onto a serving plate. Scatter over a little more parsley.

ENERGY KCAL	CARBOHYDRATE G	SUGARS G	PROTEIN G	FAT G	SATURATED FAT G	SALT G
402	2.3	2.2	31.9	29.1	12.5	2.2

Indian Masala Omelette

These thin omelettes are almost like a spicy pancake, and lend themselves to being torn into strips as you eat, or rolled around a few leaves and avocado with tzatziki. They are, however, tender and delicate, meaning your non-stick pan needs to do what it was designed for, otherwise you will end up with scrambled omelette, albeit still delicious. They are lovely both hot and cold.

MAKES 3 OMELETTES/SERVES 2

4	medium eggs
1	tablespoon lemon juice
	small pinch of saffron filaments (approx. 10), crumbled
¼	teaspoon cayenne pepper
	sea salt
2	tablespoons coarsely chopped chives
1	heaped teaspoon finely chopped medium-hot red chilli
	handful of coarsely chopped coriander
50g	cherry tomatoes, halved downwards and sliced thinly across
2	rounded teaspoons coconut oil
2	teaspoons tzatziki, to serve (optional)

Whisk the eggs in a medium bowl with the lemon juice, spices and some salt. Stir in the chives, chilli, coriander and tomatoes. Heat a generous ½ teaspoon of coconut oil in a non-stick frying pan about 24cm diameter, add a third of the mixture, and spread this over the base like a pancake using the back of a spoon to space out the ingredients evenly. Fry for 1 minute until golden on the underside and almost cooked through, then carefully loosen with a spatula and flip over, and cook the second side for about 30 seconds. Transfer to a warm plate and cook a further two omelettes in the same fashion. Accompany with tzatziki, if wished.

ENERGY KCAL	CARBOHYDRATE G	SUGARS G	PROTEIN G	FAT G	SATURATED FAT G	SALT G
203	1.2	1.2	15.0	15.0	0.5	0.5

Smoked Salmon, Lemon and Chilli Omelette

A frittata-style omelette with lots of zip – lemon, chilli and parsley together give the traditional duo of asparagus and smoked salmon a little warm weather aspiration. And, like most frittatas, it is as good cold as hot, so it's good for grazing.

SERVES 4

200g	finger-thick asparagus (trimmed weight)
6	medium eggs
½	teaspoon finely grated lemon zest, plus 1 tablespoon juice
2	teaspoons finely chopped medium-hot red chilli
4	tablespoons coarsely chopped flat-leaf parsley
100g	sliced smoked salmon, brown meat cut out, and cut into strips 3–4cm wide
2	tablespoons extra virgin olive oil

Bring a large pan of salted water to the boil. Simmer the asparagus spears for 4–5 minutes, until just tender, then drain them into a colander and pass under the cold tap to stop them cooking any further.

Whisk the eggs in a large bowl, then whisk in the lemon zest and juice, the chilli and 3 tablespoons of parsley. Gently mix in the salmon and the asparagus spears.

Preheat the grill, and also heat a 26cm non-stick frying pan with a heatproof handle over a medium heat. Add a tablespoon of oil to the pan, tip in the frittata mixture, levelling the asparagus, and cook for 3 minutes. Scatter the remaining parsley over the top of the omelette, drizzle over another tablespoon of oil and place under the grill for 3–4 minutes until golden and puffy at the sides. The omelette can be eaten hot or at room temperature.

ENERGY KCAL	CARBOHYDRATE G	SUGARS G	PROTEIN G	FAT G	SATURATED FAT G	SALT G
174	1.2	1.2	12.6	12.9	2.6	1.0

Pea and Avo Smash with Fried Eggs

Peas with avocados is strange but strangely alluring, a modern classic, that with warm blinis and eggs has brunch written all over it. Avocado oil, like the fruit itself, is full of healthy fats. I keep a small bottle for whenever I am including it in a salad or dishes such as this. While this is a good one for vegetarians, you might also like to serve it with crispy lardons or Parma ham.

SERVES 4

4	teaspoons extra virgin olive oil
4	medium eggs
8	Buckwheat Blinis (see page 22)
	cholula (hot sauce), to serve

Pea and Avo Smash

100g	shelled peas
2	tablespoons avocado oil
	sea salt
2	avocados, halved and stoned
1	tablespoon lemon juice
1	tablespoon coarsely chopped flat-leaf parsley, plus a little extra to serve

For the pea and avo smash, bring a small pan of water to the boil, add the peas and simmer for 5 minutes, then drain into a sieve. Tip into a large bowl, drizzle over the avocado oil, season with a little salt and crush them using a potato masher. Leave to cool to room temperature, then scoop out and add the avocado flesh and the lemon juice and coarsely crush, again using the potato masher. Stir in the parsley.

Heat a medium, non-stick frying pan over a medium heat, trickle 2 teaspoons of olive oil over the base, crack two eggs and fry for 2–3 minutes until lacy and crisp at the edges, basting the yolk with the hot fat until the membrane turns translucent. Transfer to a warm plate and cook the remaining eggs, adding a little more oil to the pan. At the same time, heat a second non-stick frying pan over a low heat and warm the blinis on both sides. Arrange these on plates and spread them with the pea and avo smash. Pop a fried egg on top of each pair, scatter over a little more parsley if wished, a grinding of black pepper and splash with cholula sauce.

ENERGY KCAL	CARBOHYDRATE G	SUGARS G	PROTEIN G	FAT G	SATURATED FAT G	SALT G
422	7.2	2.0	13.8	36.3	9.0	0.3

Asparagus Spears with Poached Eggs and Parmesan

Long-stem broccoli, fine green beans and asparagus are three of my default green veggies, the ones that I pick up on pretty much every food shopping foray. I realise there is a season for all of them when they are likely to be at their best, but even out of season they rarely suffer the same indignity as say strawberries, that are a completely different fruit mid-winter than in the summer. With scarcely any preparation called for, and taking just minutes to cook, there are endless ways of turning asparagus into a light lunch or supper, such as here by rolling them in the pan with a sliver of salty Normandy butter and popping a poached egg on top. And this is a good way of serving green beans and broccoli too.

SERVES 2

200g	thin asparagus spears (trimmed weight)
15g	salted butter
	slug of white wine vinegar or cider vinegar
2	medium eggs
2	tablespoons freshly grated Parmesan or mature Mimolette

Bring a large pan of salted water to the boil, add the asparagus and cook for 2–3 minutes, until the end of a spear slices through with ease. Drain into a colander, return to the pan and toss with the butter.

At the same time, bring a second large pan of water to the boil and acidulate it with a slug of vinegar. Keep it just below a simmer, stirring it into a slow whirlpool. Break the eggs, one at a time, into the water. Once they rise to the surface, trim the ragged tails of white and cook for a couple of minutes longer, so about 4 minutes in total, until set on the outside while runny within. Remove with a slotted utensil and serve on top of the buttered asparagus spears, showered with grated Parmesan or Mimolette.

ENERGY KCAL	CARBOHYDRATE G	SUGARS G	PROTEIN G	FAT G	SATURATED FAT G	SALT G
179	2.1	2.0	11.9	13.3	6.3	0.5

Broccoli and Coriander Galettes with Gravadlax

These pancakes, or galettes (a word that suits their rustic charm), are an excellent starting point for how to make a savoury pancake with a healthy profile using vegetables as the main ingredient. I would play around; cauliflower also works a treat, but over to you.

SERVES 4

250g	broccoli florets
1	heaped teaspoon chopped medium-hot green chilli
25g	coriander leaves
1	spring onion, trimmed and chopped
2	teaspoons cornflour, sifted
	sea salt
4	medium eggs
	juice of ½ lime, plus wedges to serve
approx. 1	tablespoon groundnut oil
250g	sliced gravadlax (optional)

Bring a medium pan of salted water to the boil and cook the broccoli for 5–7 minutes until tender. Drain it into a sieve, then place over a pan or bowl and press out as much liquid as possible using a potato masher. Leave to cool for about 10 minutes.

Whizz the broccoli with the chilli, coriander, spring onion, cornflour and some salt to a coarse purée in a food processor, then add the eggs and the lime juice and continue to whizz until smooth.

Heat a teaspoon of the oil in a large, non-stick frying pan over a medium heat and tilt to coat the base. Drop heaped tablespoons of the mixture into the pan, levelling the surface into a small galette or pancake 8–9cm diameter, and fry for 1–2 minutes until golden and lacy on the underside and pitted and dry on the top. Very carefully turn them by slipping a spatula underneath, and cook for a further minute or so. Transfer these to a plate and either keep warm in a very low oven (about 90°C fan/110°C electric/gas mark ¼), or cover with foil, while you cook the remainder, adding more oil to the pan as necessary.

Serve the galettes, with gravadlax if wished, accompanied by lime wedges.

ENERGY KCAL	CARBOHYDRATE G	SUGARS G	PROTEIN G	FAT G	SATURATED FAT G	SALT G
139	3.4	1.4	10.2	8.6	1.7	0.3

Skinny Mac Cheese Fritters

Edamame bean spaghetti is a personal favourite among various alternatives, and like the most delicate of Italian egg pastas, it is super skinny and tastes much like any other pasta with a similar texture. So test this one out on those diehard pasta lovers and I really don't think they will notice that it's not the finest hand-rolled fettuccine.

MAKES 8/SERVES 4

50g	edamame or soya bean spaghetti
approx. 2	tablespoons extra virgin olive oil
2	medium eggs
1	garlic clove, peeled and crushed to a paste
	sea salt, black pepper
1	tablespoon finely chopped spring onion
2	tablespoons finely chopped flat-leaf parsley
30g	freshly grated Parmesan
50g	grated Comté
150g	fine spiralised courgette
	squeeze of lemon juice
	generous handful of rocket

Bring a medium pan of salted water to the boil, add the spaghetti, give it a stir and simmer until just tender, following the packet instructions. Drain into a sieve and run it under the cold tap. Give the sieve a shake, then return the pasta to the saucepan and toss with a teaspoon of oil.

Meanwhile, whisk the eggs in a large bowl with the garlic and a generous dose of seasoning, then mix in the spring onion, parsley and Parmesan. Fold in the pasta and the grated Comté.

Heat 2 teaspoons of oil in a large, non-stick frying pan over a medium heat, give the pasta a good stir to ensure it is evenly coated, and drop a few rounded tablespoons of the mixture into the pan, flattening them into individual fritters with the back of a spatula. Fry for about 2 minutes until golden and crispy on the underside, then turn and cook the second side for a further 1–2 minutes. Drain on a double thickness of kitchen paper while you cook the remainder, adding a little more oil to the pan as necessary. You can keep them warm in a low oven (about 90°C fan/110°C electric/gas mark ¼).

Toss the courgette in a large bowl, with 1½ tablespoons of oil, a squeeze of lemon juice and a pinch of salt, and mix in the rocket. Serve this piled on top of the fritters.

ENERGY KCAL	CARBOHYDRATE G	SUGARS G	PROTEIN G	FAT G	SATURATED FAT G	SALT G
200	2.8	1.7	16.4	12.9	5.1	0.4

Cauliflower Rissoles with Beetroot Relish

As if cauliflower needed any more attention, here is yet another dish that shines the spotlight on its endless talents. Beetroot relish, lovely, but otherwise anything crisp and green.

SERVES 4

Relish

300g	cooked and peeled beetroot (unvinegared), coarsely grated
approx. 3	tablespoons extra virgin olive oil
2	teaspoons balsamic vinegar
	sea salt

Rissoles

300g	cauliflower florets
2	medium eggs
1	spring onion, trimmed and finely chopped, plus extra, finely sliced, to serve
1	rounded teaspoon finely chopped garlic
1	rounded teaspoon finely chopped fresh ginger
1	level teaspoon finely chopped medium-hot red chilli

For the relish, squeeze handfuls of the beetroot to rid it of excess juice, then place in a medium bowl. Add a tablespoon of olive oil, the vinegar and some salt and toss to mix.

For the rissoles, thinly slice the cauliflower florets using a food processing attachment. Whisk the eggs in a large bowl with the spring onion, garlic, ginger, chilli and some salt, add the cauliflower and stir to coat. The recipe can be prepared to this point well in advance, in which case cover and chill.

Heat a tablespoon of olive oil in a large, non-stick frying pan over a medium-low heat. Drop a few heaped tablespoons of the cauliflower mixture into the pan, then use a spoon or spatula to press each one down into a ragged patty about 1cm thick. Cook for 1½–2 minutes until an even lacy gold on the underside, then turn and cook for a further 1½–2 minutes until the cauliflower is tender. Transfer these to a plate lined with kitchen paper and cook the remainder in batches, adding more oil to the pan as necessary.

Serve the rissoles with a dollop of the relish, scattered with a few slivers of spring onion.

ENERGY KCAL	CARBOHYDRATE G	SUGARS G	PROTEIN G	FAT G	SATURATED FAT G	SALT G
186	9.6	8.9	7.4	12.4	2.1	0.3

Leek and Parmesan Scramble

After living for a brief time in Seville, I acquired a passion for huevos revueltos, *the artful Spanish-style of scrambled eggs, which would arrive with anything from wild asparagus to razor shell clams. But like so much apparently effortless bohemia, they are incredibly difficult to get just so. Eventually I decided that the quiet comfort of our home-style of scrambled eggs married with similar additions was the way to go. Crispy chorizo on the side and a small glass of sherry... lovely.*

SERVES 2

10g	unsalted butter
1	leek, trimmed, halved lengthways and thinly sliced
	sea salt, black pepper
3	large eggs, plus 1 extra yolk
15g	freshly grated Parmesan, plus extra to serve
1	tablespoon finely chopped walnuts
	cayenne pepper

Melt the butter in a medium, non-stick saucepan over a low heat. Fry the leek for 8–10 minutes until soft and translucent, stirring occasionally, and lightly seasoning with salt and pepper at the end.

Meanwhile, whisk the eggs and yolk with the Parmesan and a pinch of salt. Stir these into the leeks and stir constantly with a wooden spoon, covering the base of the saucepan, until thick and creamy.

Quickly divide between two small plates, scatter with the walnuts, extra Parmesan and a dusting of cayenne pepper.

ENERGY KCAL	CARBOHYDRATE G	SUGARS G	PROTEIN G	FAT G	SATURATED FAT G	SALT G
263	1.3	1.2	17.3	20.6	7.3	0.5

Noodles, Pasta and Pilafs

If the tectonic plates have shifted for the low carber of late, then the shift is captured by this chapter. And it is on two fronts, the first is the ready availability of alternative pastas, fashioned from all manner of ingredients that are low in carbohydrates and high in protein, including Asian-style noodles made with the high-fibre corms of konjac (a perennial herb, native to east Asia). So whereas our favourite pasta dishes and soupy bowls of noodles used to be off the agenda, they are now back on.

And the second change relates to an increased understanding about the role of whole grains in our diets, and the protective effect they afford in relation to the risk of bowel cancer. At face value, if we are seeking to reduce our carbohydrate intake, then excluding grains can seem like a logical step to take. Certainly there is little to be gained from refined starchy carbs like white rice and pasta, other than energy. But in their unrefined state, whole grains come packaged with a wide array of benefits, and it is much healthier to rethink their inclusion in our diet than simply cut them out entirely.

So where you will find risottos and pilafs in this chapter, these are not the classic starchy dishes that are all rice and no veg, but the opposite – with lots of vegetables and just a smattering of whole grains. This gives us the best of both worlds; the fibre in whole grains serves both to satisfy and make us feel full for longer, as well as containing about half the energy of other carbohydrates – and we are increasing our vegetable intake to boot. The fact they have lovely flavours and textures is a win-win.

In keeping with the chapter on breads, I am not suggesting that you live off these kind of dishes, but that to include them once or twice a week will broaden the range of nutrients you are getting, and in particular the type of fibre, in a way that exemplifies good nutrition. As ever, nutrition isn't about eating a lot of any one ingredient, it's about grazing on a vast smorgasbord, a little of this, a little of that.

Noodles Reinvented

A noodle that has zero calories seems too good to be true. And yet if you pop into any health food store these days you will find a variety of brands selling pasta and rice with just those credentials. So how does that work? The Japanese are no strangers to konjac and the thin noodles that can be made with it, which are labelled as shirataki or yam noodles. The main components are water and glucomannan, a type of low-carb, low-fat, water-soluble dietary fibre, so there are next to no calories attached. Shirataki noodles have the kind of gelatinous texture that is not untypical in Asian cooking, and that fits neatly within the character of a deep noodle pot or stir-fry. But at the risk of being a grinch, I am less convinced about their reinvention as classic pasta shapes such as penne, spaghetti and fettuccine, as well as rice.

Cooking tips

Shirataki noodles typically on sale are stored in what might politely be described as an 'odiferous' liquid, but it does disperse with a thorough rinse and simmering for a little longer than is recommended. Dry-frying the noodles after washing and drying is another good ruse that modifies their texture and they become, dare I say it, a little more Italian. If these noodles do become a regular part of your repertoire, then there are an increasing number of brands and it is worth working your way through several to find the one that cooks up to your liking.

Cooking tips

As with shirataki noodles, if high-protein noodles are likely to make a regular appearance on your table, then I would suggest trying a few different types and adopt a brand that you like. But, in terms of what to look for, the Liberto brand stands out as leading the way in quality. High-protein noodles benefit from being left al dente, about 3 minutes cooking should be enough; they tend to be delicate and can start to break up and cling together given too long. So start checking a minute or two before the suggested cooking time on the packet.

Pasta Reinvented

It was however, only a matter of time before some driven genius came up with a pasta that was low in carbs. The latest newcomers are high-protein noodles made with ingredients such as soya and edamame beans. Again, these are not typical of classic pastas, a rough cousin beside their silken Italian relatives, and a flavour of their own. I wouldn't say they are a direct swap but, with a judicious choice of sauce they cook up a treat, and a pan of noodles dressed with olive oil, chilli, garlic and anchovies is one that has me going back for more. They also take kindly to being dressed with pesto.

Such noodles swell to several times their weight, so less are needed than a classic pasta. And their high protein content also allows for a small portion, as they satisfy in the same way as a steak for supper.

Whereas classic durum wheat pasta gulps up any available moisture after it is drained, these noodles are positively aloof by comparison, and without absorbing so much as a drop of the cooking liquid, remain pert and waxy even once cool. So firstly, give them a thorough shake when draining so as not to dilute the sauce, and secondly, hang on to the leftovers which will still be on fine form the following day. Cooking up a dish of pasta to feed four when there are only two of you will reap the reward of yummy salad noodles to graze on.

Whole Grains

Possibly the greatest challenge for nutritionists advising us to eat up our starchy unrefined carbs is keeping pace with changing tastes. We have known for decades that brown bread is better for us than white, or whole wheat pasta and brown rice preferable to refined. And yet our consumption of these foods continues to fall. But is this such a surprise, given how heavy these foods are in terms of palatability and the sensation that follows on eating them? So when whole grains are delivered as a substantial aside to a stew or sauce, for many people who have come to relish the light and seductive textures associated with vegetables, fruit, cheeses, chicken and fish, they turn away. Add to this a general distrust of starchy carbohydrates and it is a perfect storm of refusal to eat them.

Before studying to become a nutritionist, I numbered myself among that group. But with a better understanding of the role that whole grains play I wanted to find a way of addressing the problem. I am convinced that the answer is to reappraise how we include these foods in our lives, rather than excluding them. You don't need to give whole grains the entire stage; instead, treat them as you would an incidental ingredient such as olives, or sun-dried tomatoes, adding them to a dish as a smattering, and they are reborn. It could be a salad of tomatoes, cucumber and avocado with lots of herbs, lemon and pomegranate seeds, and just a sprinkling of cooked spelt grains or buckwheat. Suddenly they acquire an allure, with their comforting mealy texture meeting the succulent freshness of the salad. And it's not just salads, there is no reason why a pilaf shouldn't be as much vegetable as grain, or, if you do want to serve them as an aside, then cut them with lots of other tasty veg.

The range of whole grains available seems to get better with every year that passes; spelt, buckwheat, farro, even quinoa comes in different colours today. At a popular level whole grains have taken over where pulses left off. This is partly their convenience, most take 15–20 minutes to cook, and also come in pouches ready-prepared. So let's revisit them and harness the goodness they have to offer.

Pulses

The new high-protein noodles answer the need to consume legumes, and we also have recourse to the most fashionable bean of all, edamame. On that note, one of my favourite freezer conveniences is a bag of frozen soya beans (i.e. edamame beans) that are altogether fresher and greener than the little pots nestling up to the pomegranate seeds and seaweed thins by way of a convenient snack food. Lentils are another exception among pulses, being high in protein, and less carby than other types. They vie for whole grain status and I tend to use them in the same way, they have a lovely bite and aroma and can be used as you might nuts in a dish, just a little will be more enticing than a large plateful.

A broad range of low carb, gluten-free pastas is available from Holland & Barrett (www.hollandandbarrett.com).

Miso Noodles with Prawns and Choi Sum

Like so many Asian dishes this is all about a last-minute flurry of activity, so have everything weighed out and at the ready. Ultimately, it's a three-tiered bowl of silky white konjac noodles, crisp greens and succulent prawns. Young rainbow chard offers up another leafy green – simply slice across the leaves and fry these up with the sliced stalks.

SERVES 2

150g	raw shelled king prawns
1	tablespoon sesame or groundnut oil
200g	konjac noodles, drained and well- rinsed
100g	choi sum, sliced 1cm thick
7g	dried arame (or other sea vegetable), soaked in cold water for 15 minutes and drained
1	tablespoon teriyaki sauce
1	tablespoon sesame seeds
	generous squeeze of lemon or lime juice
1	level tablespoon brown miso (e.g. barley or rice)
200ml	boiling water
1	spring onion, trimmed and thinly sliced diagonally
	chilli oil (optional)

Rinse the prawns in a sieve and pat dry between sheets of kitchen paper. Toss in a small bowl with a teaspoon of the oil.

Heat a large, non-stick frying pan over a medium-high heat for several minutes, add the drained noodles and dry-fry for 3–5 minutes, stirring frequently, then divide them between a couple of warm, deep soup bowls. Add a couple of teaspoons of oil to the pan and stir-fry the choi sum for about 1 minute, then add the seaweed and teriyaki sauce and cook for a minute longer. Stir in the sesame seeds and spoon on top of the noodles. Now stir-fry the prawns for about 2 minutes until pink and firm, squeeze over a little lemon or lime juice and scatter these over the vegetables and noodles.

Place the miso in a measuring jug and gradually work in the boiling water. Pour over the assembled ingredients and scatter with some spring onion strips. A dash of chilli oil peps things up nicely if you have some in the cupboard.

ENERGY KCAL	CARBOHYDRATE G	SUGARS G	PROTEIN G	FAT G	SATURATED FAT G	SALT G
194	5.5	2.3	16.5	10.7	1.6	2.7

Spaghetti with Roast Asparagus

Asparagus is the heart and soul of any party. Dispensing with the need for acolytes, its scent takes care of a plate of noodles with little call for much else, aside from a generous addition of Parmesan and some parsley.

SERVES 4

350–400g	thin asparagus, ends trimmed, and cut into 3–4cm pieces
2	tablespoons extra virgin olive oil
	sea salt, black pepper
3	garlic cloves, peeled and finely chopped
1	teaspoon finely chopped medium-hot red chilli
130g	edamame bean spaghetti
2	tablespoons lemon juice
50g	freshly grated Parmesan, plus extra, finely shaved, to serve
2	handfuls of coarsely chopped flat-leaf parsley

Preheat the oven to 190°C fan/210°C electric/gas mark 6½. Arrange the asparagus in a crowded layer in a large roasting pan, drizzle over the olive oil, season and toss to coat it. Roast for 15 minutes, then stir in the garlic and chilli and continue to roast for a further 10 minutes until really soft and lightly coloured.

Meanwhile, bring a large pan of salted water to the boil. Add the spaghetti, give it a stir to separate out the strands and simmer until just tender – check a minute or so earlier than the packet instructions advise. Reserving half a teacup of the cooking liquid, drain the pasta into a colander, then tip it into the asparagus roasting pan, drizzle over the lemon juice, scatter over the grated Parmesan and a little more seasoning. Drizzle over the reserved cooking liquid, place the pan over a gentle heat and stir constantly until the pasta is coated in a creamy emulsion. Stir in the parsley and serve scattered with fine shavings of Parmesan.

ENERGY KCAL	CARBOHYDRATE G	SUGARS G	PROTEIN G	FAT G	SATURATED FAT G	SALT G
256	7.3	4.6	21.9	13.3	3.7	0.2

Edamame Fettuccine with Salsa Crudo

Edamame bean noodles are very at home in this robust and earthy pasta dish. Treat it as a basic and spread the pleasure with Parmesan shavings, crumbled feta, chopped walnuts, toasted pine nuts and the like. You can use any edamame-style noodle here, though the ideal will be on the short side, some 4–5cm long, so maybe break them if they are much longer than that.

SERVES 2

150g	very ripe cherry tomatoes, thinly sliced
	sea salt, black pepper
1	heaped tablespoon finely chopped shallot
1	tablespoon finely chopped medium-hot red chilli
75g	edamame and mung bean fettuccine
2	tablespoons extra virgin olive oil
2	teaspoons balsamic vinegar
2	teaspoons lemon juice
4	heaped tablespoons finely chopped flat-leaf parsley, plus extra to serve

Place the tomatoes in a large bowl, season generously with salt, then mix in the shallot and chilli and set aside.

Bring a medium pan of salted water to the boil, add the fettuccine to the pan, stir to separate the strands and cook until just tender – check a minute or so earlier than the packet instructions advise. Drain the pasta into a sieve or colander quite thoroughly.

Add the olive oil, balsamic vinegar, lemon juice and parsley to the tomatoes and stir. Add the drained pasta and toss to mix. Season to taste with a little more salt and some black pepper, and serve scattered with a little extra parsley.

ENERGY KCAL	CARBOHYDRATE G	SUGARS G	PROTEIN G	FAT G	SATURATED FAT G	SALT G
274	9.0	6.3	17.6	16.1	2.3	trace

Rainbow Spaghetti with Parmesan, Parsley and Crispy Bacon

I confess to being swept up by spiraliser-mania and the delicious vegetable noodles that result, along with many others. I also confess that the ingenious contraption I have for the task is now collecting dust at the back of a deep cupboard. It is a brilliant design that folds down to a small discreet box, the issue being that it requires the skill of a 10-year old whizz at Lego to assemble and I don't use it often enough to remember how to do it. So during those minutes spent scratching my head and working out is that a shaft or is it the handle, I could have done it by hand.

But, I am not giving up, because if you do want to go down this route, and this dish is a very good advertisement for spiralised veggies, then they are infinitely better made at home than bought. Like other pre-prepared vegetables, they rapidly succumb to drying and browning where they are cut, and there is no way of trimming them. So I won't be throwing my spiraliser out just yet.

SERVES 2

80g	unsmoked streaky bacon, cut into 1cm dice, or lardons
30g	salted butter
1	small garlic clove, peeled and crushed to a paste
	sea salt, black pepper
300g	courgette noodles (3mm)
100g	carrot noodles (3mm)
2	tablespoons finely chopped flat-leaf parsley, plus extra to serve
50g	freshly grated Parmesan
1	tablespoon extra virgin olive oil
	lemon wedges, to serve

Gently heat the bacon in a large, non-stick frying pan over a medium heat, and fry in the rendered fat for 4–7 minutes until golden and crisp, stirring frequently. Transfer to a double thickness of kitchen paper to drain.

Bring a large (unsalted) pan of water to the boil. Melt the butter with the garlic and some seasoning in a small saucepan.

Add the noodles to the boiling water, blanch for 1 minute, then drain into a colander and shake dry for about 30 seconds. Return these to the saucepan, pour over the garlic butter, scatter over the parsley and half the Parmesan and toss to coat.

Divide between two shallow soup bowls. Scatter over the remaining Parmesan, a little more parsley and the bacon, then drizzle over some olive oil. Accompany with lemon wedges.

ENERGY KCAL	CARBOHYDRATE G	SUGARS G	PROTEIN G	FAT G	SATURATED FAT G	SALT G
336	6.6	6.2	9.6	28.9	12.2	1.6

Spaghetti with Anchovies, Garlic and Parsley

A lively, uncooked sauce that can be thrown together in the time it takes to bring a pan of water to the boil. A little garlic is optional and gives the sauce more bite, but for a late morning brunch, for instance, you might want to forego this. Also, being a raw sauce, a really good oil will shine. Black soya bean spaghetti is ideal with any sauce containing fish, redolent of black squid ink, but any high protein noodle such as edamame bean can be used as well.

SERVES 2

100g black soya bean spaghetti

Sauce

5 tablespoons extra virgin olive oil, plus extra to serve

juice of ½ lemon

1 garlic clove, peeled and crushed to a paste (optional)

2 teaspoons finely chopped medium-hot red chilli

8 salted anchovy fillets, thinly sliced

4 tablespoons finely chopped flat-leaf parsley, plus extra to serve

Bring a large pan of salted water to the boil, and combine the ingredients for the sauce in a large bowl. Add the spaghetti to the pan, stir to separate the strands and cook until just tender – check a minute or so earlier than the packet instructions advise. Drain the pasta into a sieve or colander quite thoroughly, then toss with the sauce in the bowl, and serve drizzled with extra olive oil and scattered with a little more parsley.

ENERGY KCAL	CARBOHYDRATE G	SUGARS G	PROTEIN G	FAT G	SATURATED FAT G	SALT G
484	7.4	3.8	25.3	36.8	5.2	1.2

Spinach and Noodles with Mint Yogurt

This spinach and noodle dish is more Turkish than Italian, and relies on the boost of a mélange of spices and a fresh mint yogurt to afford it character, rather than Parmesan. This requires a little more work than many of the recipes in the book, more relaxed supper than speedy lunch, but it's not overly onerous and still within the 30-minute time frame.

SERVES 4

2	tablespoons extra virgin olive oil
20g	unsalted butter
3	banana shallots, peeled, halved and thinly sliced
1	celery heart, trimmed and thinly sliced
3	garlic cloves, peeled and finely sliced
¼	teaspoon ground allspice
¼	teaspoon ground cinnamon
125ml	white wine
	sea salt, black pepper
	freshly grated nutmeg
500g	spinach, washed*
75g	edamame and mung bean, or black soya bean, fettuccine
	sumac
4	tablespoons roast cashews, coarsely crushed (optional), to serve

Yogurt

75g	feta
150g	0%-fat Greek yogurt
1	teaspoon lemon juice
1	heaped tablespoon finely chopped mint

You will need to cook the vegetable base, the spinach and put the water on for the noodles at the same time. Start by heating the oil and half the butter in a medium-large saucepan over a low heat. Fry the shallots and celery for about 15 minutes until golden, stirring occasionally, adding the garlic, allspice and cinnamon a couple of minutes before the end. Add the wine, turn the heat up and simmer until well-reduced and syrupy. Season generously with salt, pepper and nutmeg.

Put the washed spinach in a large saucepan, cover with a lid and steam over a gentle heat for 10 minutes until it collapses, stirring halfway through. Tip it into a colander and press out the excess water using a potato masher or the back of a ladle. Mix this into the vegetable base.

Add the fettuccine to the pan of boiling water shortly before the base is ready, stir to separate the strands and cook until just tender – check a minute or so earlier than the packet instructions advise. Drain the pasta into a sieve or colander, shaking off the excess water. Return to the pan and toss with the remaining butter.

While the vegetables and pasta are cooking, prepare the yogurt. Coarsely mash the feta with the yogurt in a small bowl, and stir in the lemon juice and mint.

Place a pile of vegetables on four plates, with a small pile of noodles to the side. Dollop the feta yogurt on top of the spinach and dust everything with sumac. If wished you can also scatter with nuts.

*Even if the spinach advertises it has been washed, pass the leaves under a cold tap in a colander – the water that clings to the leaves results in it steaming.

ENERGY KCAL	CARBOHYDRATE G	SUGARS G	PROTEIN G	FAT G	SATURATED FAT G	SALT G
397	10.3	6.7	22.9	24.5	7.9	1.1

Roast Asparagus and Red Onion with Farro

This accommodating little dish is ideal for when you are not completely sure about when you might sit down to eat; served hot, ambient or cool it will still be lovely. And, should you be feeling particularly hungry, it welcomes a lightly poached egg, or some griddled and sliced chicken. Conveniently, most farro sold today is quick-cook and takes less than 15 minutes, a boon for a grain.

SERVES 4

1	tablespoon lemon juice
1	garlic clove, peeled and crushed to a paste
approx. 3	tablespoons extra virgin olive oil
350–400g	fine asparagus, ends trimmed and halved
	sea salt, black pepper
2	red onions, peeled, halved and thinly sliced across
50g	farro
1	tablespoon small (non-pareil) capers, rinsed
	handful of coarsely chopped flat-leaf parsley
	chia seeds, for scattering (optional)
	lemon wedges, to serve

Preheat the oven to 190°C fan/210°C electric/gas mark 6½. Combine the lemon juice and garlic with 2 tablespoons of olive oil in a large bowl. Add the asparagus and toss to coat, then season well and spread over the base of a large roasting pan. Spread the onion over a baking sheet, separating out the slices, drizzle over a little oil and toss to coat them. Roast the asparagus for about 20 minutes until lightly golden, and roast the onion for 25 minutes, stirring it around halfway through to ensure it caramelises evenly.

Meanwhile, bring a medium pan of salted water to the boil and cook the farro for 15 minutes or until just tender. Drain into a sieve.

Stir the farro and onion into the asparagus, then mix in the capers and taste for seasoning. Transfer to a serving dish and eat hot or at room temperature, stirring in the parsley at the last minute, and scattering with chia seeds, if wished. Accompany with lemon wedges.

ENERGY KCAL	CARBOHYDRATE G	SUGARS G	PROTEIN G	FAT G	SATURATED FAT G	SALT G
186	15.4	6.2	5.6	10.5	1.5	0.2

Salad of Buckwheat, Watercress, Coriander and Avocado

The inclusion of buckwheat in this dish takes its cue from tabbouleh, where only a smattering of bulgar wheat features among a mass of juicy leaves and tomatoes. The idea being that the buckwheat (in fact a pseudograin) is in balance with all the other ingredients and in the same proportion, without any hint of being stodgy or overwhelming. And buckwheat is lovely stuff, so pretty with its neat architectural sides and corners.

SERVES 4

Salad

40g	buckwheat
150g	cherry tomatoes, halved
	sea salt, black pepper
75g	watercress
	large handful of coarsely chopped coriander
75g	pitted dry black olives, halved
2	spring onions, trimmed and thinly sliced
1	large avocado, halved and stoned

Dressing

2	teaspoons balsamic vinegar
1	teaspoon lemon juice
2	tablespoons avocado oil

For the salad, bring a medium pan of salted water to the boil, add the buckwheat and simmer for 15 minutes or until just tender, then drain into a sieve and set aside to cool. Meanwhile, toss the tomatoes with a little salt in a medium bowl and set aside for 15 minutes.

Slice the pile of watercress into 3–4cm lengths and combine with the coriander, olives, spring onions and buckwheat in a large bowl.

To make the dressing, whisk the vinegar and lemon juice with a little seasoning in a small bowl, then stir in the avocado oil.

Slice the avocado into thin strips lengthways in the skin, then run a spoon between the skin and the flesh to scoop these out into the bowl with the tomatoes. Pour the dressing over the tomatoes and avocado and gently stir. (You can prepare the salad to this point about 30 minutes in advance.) Spoon the tomatoes and avocado over the buckwheat salad and gently toss, then serve.

ENERGY KCAL	CARBOHYDRATE G	SUGARS G	PROTEIN G	FAT G	SATURATED FAT G	SALT G
264	10.9	2.6	3.4	21.6	3.2	1.0

Asparagus and Spelt Risotto with Crab

Light and soupy, this is as much about asparagus and leeks as it is the grains of pearled spelt. The crab provides a little high-end glamour, but this could be prawns or flakes of salmon, also crumbled feta or a young goat's cheese. Chia seeds have a cameo role here, to help provide body to the risotto and lightly thicken the juices further.

SERVES 6

100g	pearled spelt
300g	fine asparagus, ends trimmed
3	tablespoons extra virgin olive oil
300g	leeks (trimmed weight), halved lengthways and thinly sliced
1	garlic clove, peeled and finely chopped
100ml	white wine
2	level tablespoons chia seeds
	finely grated zest of 1 lemon, plus 1 tablespoon juice
500ml	vegetable stock
	sea salt, black pepper
10g	unsalted butter
200g	mixed brown and white crabmeat

Bring a small pan of salted water to the boil, add the spelt and simmer for 20 minutes or until just tender. Drain into a sieve and set aside.

Meanwhile, cut off and reserve the asparagus tips, and finely slice the stalks. Heat 2 tablespoons of olive oil in a large saucepan and fry the leeks and garlic for about 5 minutes until softened and glossy, without colouring, stirring occasionally. Stir in the sliced asparagus, add the wine and simmer to reduce by half. Stir in the chia seeds and the lemon zest, add the stock and some seasoning, bring to the boil and simmer for 5–8 minutes until the vegetables are tender. Stir in the spelt and taste for seasoning.

While the risotto base is cooking, bring a small pan of salted water to the boil, add the asparagus tips and simmer for 3–4 minutes or until just tender. Drain into a sieve, return to the pan and toss with the butter. Dress the crab with a tablespoon each of olive oil and lemon juice and lightly season. Serve the risotto in bowls with the crab spooned on top, and the asparagus tips scattered over.

ENERGY KCAL	CARBOHYDRATE G	SUGARS G	PROTEIN G	FAT G	SATURATED FAT G	SALT G
232	11.1	2.3	12.2	11.1	2.3	0.8

Spicy Courgette and Quinoa Pilaf

Fresh turmeric root has a fabulously intense colour and is altogether more subtle than dried. And, like ginger, it has a chameleon-like ability to blend with all manner of flavour palates. Just a small word of caution: it dyes everything it comes into contact with in a way that makes beetroot seem shy. Definitely not something to do in your whites.

SERVES 4

	flesh of 2 medium avocados
2–3	teaspoons lime juice, plus wedges to serve
	sea salt, black pepper
600g	courgettes, ends trimmed, halved lengthways and sliced 1.5cm thick
4	tablespoons extra virgin olive oil
2 x 4–5cm	fresh turmeric roots, peeled
3cm	knob of fresh ginger, peeled
1	teaspoon finely chopped medium-hot red chilli
2	garlic cloves, peeled
1 x 250g	packet 'ready-to-eat' quinoa (e.g. red and white), crumbled to separate the grains
	large handful of coarsely chopped coriander, plus a little extra to serve
30g	pine nuts

Preheat the oven to 230°C fan/250°C electric/gas mark 9½. Whizz the avocado flesh with the lime juice to taste and some seasoning. Scoop into a small bowl, cover and chill until required. Arrange the sliced courgettes over the base of a large roasting pan that holds it in a crowded layer. Drizzle over 2 tablespoons of oil, season and toss to coat. Roast for 15 minutes, stirring halfway through.

In the meantime, whizz the turmeric, ginger, chilli and garlic to a coarse paste in a food processor. Transfer to a small bowl and add a tablespoon of oil. Loosen the courgettes with a spatula, dot with the paste and stir to coat. Return to the oven for a further 10–15 minutes until lightly golden.

Spoon the quinoa over the courgettes, which will warm the grain. Drizzle over the remaining tablespoon of oil and stir, then mix in the coriander. Serve the avocado dolloped on top of the pilaf, scattered with pine nuts and a little more coriander. Accompany with lime wedges.

ENERGY KCAL	CARBOHYDRATE G	SUGARS G	PROTEIN G	FAT G	SATURATED FAT G	SALT G
414	14.9	4.7	9.7	33.2	5.7	trace

Mushroom, Fromage Frais and Buckwheat Risotto

I have developed a bit of a crush on buckwheat and it is conveniently lower in carbs than most whole grains, with lots of fibre and protein. It manages to be tender, sweet and nutty all at the same time. The mushroom sauce takes care of the creamy texture we expect of a risotto, and the inclusion of some dried wild ones raises the bar. It is also possible to find a quick-cook buckwheat which is ready in 5 minutes and cooks using the absorption method.

SERVES 4

15g	dried wild mushrooms
150ml	boiling water
300ml	chicken or vegetable stock
60g	buckwheat
2	tablespoons extra virgin olive oil, plus extra to serve
10g	unsalted butter
200g	leeks (trimmed weight), halved lengthways and thinly sliced
400g	mixed mushrooms, trimmed and torn or sliced as necessary
1	garlic clove, peeled and finely chopped
100ml	white wine
	sea salt, black pepper
150g	low-fat fromage frais
	coarsely chopped flat-leaf parsley, to serve
	freshly grated Parmesan (about 1 tablespoon)

Cover the wild mushrooms with the boiling water and leave them to soak for 15 minutes. Remove and coarsely chop the mushrooms, then add the soaking liquor to the stock, discarding the last little gritty bit.

Bring a medium pan of salted water to the boil, add the buckwheat and simmer for 15 minutes or until just tender, and then drain into a colander.

Meanwhile, heat half the oil with the butter in a large saucepan over a medium-high heat and fry the leek for 2–3 minutes until soft, then transfer to a bowl. Add the remaining oil to the pan and fry the mushrooms for about 5 minutes until lightly coloured, stirring frequently, and adding the garlic shortly before the end. If they give out any liquid while frying, simply continue to cook until this evaporates. Add the soaked mushrooms and the wine and simmer for a couple of minutes until well-reduced. Add the stock and some seasoning, and bring to the boil.

Remove half the mushrooms with a slotted spoon to the bowl with the leeks, and purée the remaining mushrooms and liquid with the fromage frais in a blender until smooth. Return this to the pan, stir the reserved mushrooms and the buckwheat into the base. It is fine to briefly re-warm, but avoid simmering. Serve scattered with parsley, with a drizzle of oil, accompanied by Parmesan.

ENERGY KCAL	CARBOHYDRATE G	SUGARS G	PROTEIN G	FAT G	SATURATED FAT G	SALT G
231	15.5	3.4	11.4	11.1	3.3	0.4

Protein Pots

Protein pots are one of the better fast foods to have colonised takeaway outlets in recent years; all the good bits about the sandwich without the bread and butter. That said, I do find a plastic pot with a lonely boiled egg and just a few leaves of spinach for company a little sad. They have much more potential than that, and there seems every reason for making them a mainstay for the way we eat at home as well as when we are out. The majority can be amassed from easy ingredients, readily snatched on a whizz round the shops, and served with perhaps a simple dressing. Many can be made in advance, or the day before, and are happy to languish in a lunchbox if you are going to work.

As their name suggests, the point of these pots is to get a little protein in there, not a full-on hit the size of a burger or chicken fillet, but a small something to take the edge off your appetite in a wholesome way. It is the perfect occasion to get some fish into the equation, that doesn't require cooking, so hot- and cold-smoked salmon or mackerel, crab, prawns and crayfish are all goers. Young cheeses are also ideal, and any cold ham or chicken too, so a good use for the leftover roast.

While protein pot suggests a dinky tub for one, they lend themselves to various styles of presentation. You could arrange the ingredients as a salad, and cocktail or mini sundae dishes are another way to go, at which point they will stand as the first course for an informal lunch or supper, in prawn cocktail fashion. Personally, I appreciate them most for serving as an excuse to eat a few of my favourite things. After all, when you home in on a sandwich for lunch, for the most part your choice depends on the treasures within rather than what's around it.

Two Salmon and Guacamole Cocktail

A seriously indulgent and deluxe pot. Unable to choose between silky, transparently fine slices of smoked salmon and succulent flakes of hot-smoked fillet, here the two vie for attention beside fine asparagus spears and a guacamole laced with fresh mint and lemon. A slice of the Coconut Almond Bread (see page 18) would join it in the comfort zone.

SERVES 6

Pot

250g	thin asparagus spears, trimmed
100g	smoked salmon, cut into strips 3–4cm wide
200g	hot-smoked salmon, coarsely flaked

Guacamole

	flesh of 3 avocados
10g	mint leaves
1½	tablespoons lemon juice
1	tablespoon extra virgin olive oil
1	heaped teaspoon chopped shallot
	sea salt, black pepper

For the pot, bring a large pan of salted water to the boil, add the asparagus and cook for 3–4 minutes until just tender, then drain into a colander, refresh under the cold tap and leave to cool. Whizz all the ingredients for the guacamole to a smooth purée in a food processor. (The recipe can be prepared to this point a couple of hours in advance, in which case cover the surface of the guacamole and chill.)

You can arrange the ingredients on a large serving plate, in small bowls, or even cocktail glasses for a light lunch or first course. For the prettiest rendition, stand a small bunch of asparagus spears in six 250ml cocktail glasses, and dollop a generous heaped tablespoon of the guacamole in the centre. Arrange a couple of smoked salmon strips in a pile to one side, with some of the flaked salmon in another pile.

ENERGY KCAL	CARBOHYDRATE G	SUGARS G	PROTEIN G	FAT G	SATURATED FAT G	SALT G
262	1.8	1.7	14.7	20.8	4.6	1.2

Smoked Mackerel with Pickled Cucumber and Avocado

Pea shoots and lamb's lettuce both make for a particularly tender salad base, the perfect match for the delicacy of the smoked mackerel. With the leaves, cucumber and avocado, you have three types of veg in one pot, as well as lots of healthy fats.

SERVES 4

Pot

4	small handfuls of pea shoots or lamb's lettuce
200g	smoked mackerel, skinned and coarsely flaked

Relish

½	cucumber, peeled, quartered and thinly sliced
	sea salt
1	tablespoon extra virgin olive oil
1	tablespoon lemon juice
1	heaped teaspoon finely chopped medium-hot red chilli
1	avocado, quartered, skinned and cut into 1cm dice
1	tablespoon coarsely chopped flat-leaf parsley, plus extra to serve

For the relish, toss the cucumber with a little salt in a medium bowl and set aside for 15 minutes. Drain into a sieve, rinse under the cold tap and pat dry on a double thickness of kitchen paper. Toss with the olive oil, lemon juice and chilli in a medium bowl, and gently mix in the avocado and parsley.

For the pot, half-fill four small bowls with pea shoots or lamb's lettuce and mix in the smoked mackerel. Spoon the relish and dressing on top and scatter over a little more parsley.

ENERGY KCAL	CARBOHYDRATE G	SUGARS G	PROTEIN G	FAT G	SATURATED FAT G	SALT G
264	1.7	1.3	12.2	22.5	4.6	1.0

Salmon, Edamame and Arame Pot with Wasabi Dressing

More than a nod in the direction of Japan with seaweed, edamame beans and a spicy dressing pepped up with wasabi. Dried seaweeds are just starting to take up their place as a store cupboard staple and this is the sort of recipe for which a packet of arame (kelp) comes in handy. Not surprisingly, seaweeds are at their best in the company of fish, and work especially well with this oriental flavour palate.

SERVES 2

Pot

2	large pinches of dried arame
4	heaped tablespoons alfalfa sprouts or mustard and cress
100g	cooked salmon fillet, skinned and coarsely flaked
2	heaped tablespoons edamame beans
	sesame seeds, for sprinkling

Dressing

¾	teaspoon wasabi paste
1	teaspoon runny honey
1	teaspoon dark soy sauce (e.g. Kikkoman)
1	teaspoon sesame oil
1	tablespoon lime juice
1	tablespoon rapeseed oil

For the pot, put the arame in a medium bowl, cover with cold water and soak for 10–15 minutes, then drain into a sieve and pat dry on a double thickness of kitchen paper. Whisk together all the ingredients for the dressing in a small bowl.

Make a base of alfalfa sprouts or mustard and cress in two small bowls or pots. Pile the salmon on top, then scatter over the arame, edamame beans and some sesame seeds. (The pots can be prepared a few hours in advance, in which case cover and chill until needed). Drizzle over the dressing to serve.

ENERGY KCAL	CARBOHYDRATE G	SUGARS G	PROTEIN G	FAT G	SATURATED FAT G	SALT G
221	4.9	3.1	13.7	15.6	1.9	0.7

Quail Eggs, Crab and Cress

The peppery sauce rouille provides the foundation for a garlic mayonnaise that spars nicely with watercress. White crabmeat is the pinnacle of luxury, but I also relish brown meat for its creamy texture and deep flavour – it may not be as attractive, but it's worth bearing in mind.

SERVES 4

4	heaped teaspoons rouille
4	heaped teaspoons mayonnaise
200g	white crabmeat (or half white, half brown)
2	punnets of mustard and cress, cut
2	small handfuls of watercress sprigs
12	quail eggs, hard-boiled, peeled and halved (see page 187)
8	antipasti artichoke wedges (e.g. Sacla), drained

Combine the rouille and mayonnaise, and mix half of this with the crabmeat in a medium bowl.

Fill four small bowls with a mixture of mustard and cress and watercress. Place a spoonful of crabmeat to one side of each, three quail eggs in the middle, add a couple of artichoke wedges, then dollop a heaped teaspoon of the remaining sauce in the centre.

ENERGY KCAL	CARBOHYDRATE G	SUGARS G	PROTEIN G	FAT G	SATURATED FAT G	SALT G
245	0.6	0.6	14.4	20.5	2.4	0.5

Egg and Cress Sundae

I have to stop myself reaching for the mayonnaise when I am snacking on quail eggs, but add some cress and there is more of an excuse to indulge, and it's such a great combination.

SERVES 6

75g	mayonnaise
50g	soured cream
	sea salt
2	dozen quail eggs, hard-boiled, peeled and halved (see page 187)
2	punnets of mustard and cress, cut
50g	small watercress sprigs
	finely chopped chives
12	Sesame Parmesan Crackers (see page 21)

Combine the mayonnaise and soured cream in a medium bowl and season with a pinch of salt. Reserving 12 halves (i.e. 6 eggs), fold the remaining quail eggs into the sauce.

Combine the mustard and cress and watercress and half-fill six small bowls. Spoon the quail egg mayonnaise on top, then garnish each one with a couple of the reserved egg halves. Scatter with chives, and, tuck a couple of crackers in the side. Serve within the hour.

ENERGY KCAL	CARBOHYDRATE G	SUGARS G	PROTEIN G	FAT G	SATURATED FAT G	SALT G
171	0.7	0.6	5.8	16.1	3.2	0.1

Skinny Prawn Cocktail

A generous helping of salad veg, and a whizzed-up Sauce Marie Rose that is deceptively unctuous and like the real thing, despite its reliance on a low-fat fromage frais. Jars of mayo tend to come up quite salty and sometimes acerbic too, so diluting these traits is never a bad thing.

SERVES 4

Salad

400g	cooked and peeled cold-water prawns
½	cucumber, trimmed, quartered lengthways and thinly sliced
150g	radishes, trimmed and thinly sliced
1	tablespoon extra virgin olive oil
	squeeze of lemon juice
	small Little Gem or Romaine lettuce heart leaves – enough to serve four
2	tablespoons small (non-pareil) capers, rinsed

Sauce Marie Rose

100g	low-fat fromage frais
1	tablespoon mayonnaise
1	tablespoon tomato ketchup
	sea salt

Combine all the ingredients for the sauce in a medium bowl and fold in the prawns. Toss the cucumber and radishes with the olive oil and lemon juice in a large bowl. (You can prepare the cocktail to this point a few hours in advance, in which case cover and chill.)

Season the cucumber and radish salad with a little salt. Arrange the leaves on four plates, spoon over the salad, then top with the prawns and capers.

ENERGY KCAL	CARBOHYDRATE G	SUGARS G	PROTEIN G	FAT G	SATURATED FAT G	SALT G
168	4.9	4.8	18.7	7.6	0.9	2.0

Prawn Guacamolies

This has half an avocado as its foundation, which is piled with a generous mound of prawn salad, and finished with a soured cream sauce. Everything you would hope to find in guacamole along with the best bits about those seventies filled avocados. This version of Sauce Marie Rose is a tad richer, and sharper-tasting, than the previous one.

SERVES 4

Salad

200g	cherry tomatoes, halved
	sea salt
2	large ripe avocados
400g	cooked and peeled king prawns
2	medium-hot red chillies, cored, deseeded and cut into fine strips 3–4cm long
2	tablespoons lemon juice
2	tablespoons extra virgin olive oil
4	tablespoons finely chopped coriander, plus extra to serve

Sauce Marie Rose

100g	soured cream
2	teaspoons tomato ketchup
	shake of Tabasco

Season the tomatoes with salt in a large bowl and set aside for 15–20 minutes, the juices will enhance the dressing.

Meanwhile, blend all the ingredients for the sauce in a medium bowl with a pinch of salt.

Halve the avocados and remove the stones, then incise the skin in half and peel this off. Place an avocado half on each plate, hole upwards. Mix the prawns and chilli into the tomatoes, then toss with the lemon juice and olive oil, and fold in the coriander. Pile this on top of the avocado halves, drizzle over the sauce and scatter with a little more coriander.

ENERGY KCAL	CARBOHYDRATE G	SUGARS G	PROTEIN G	FAT G	SATURATED FAT G	SALT G
384	4.8	4.6	26.5	27.3	7.4	0.9

Southeast Asian Prawns
with Salad Greens

Sprightly, feisty and crisp, this is a sort of prawn cocktail without the creamy sauce. Asian salad greens are more robust than European ones, to be attacked with gusto. And rather than soft cold-water prawns, these need to be equally fit and toned, so a firm king prawn is ideal.

SERVES 4

Salad

400g	cooked and peeled king prawns
¼	head of Chinese leaves (top leafy section), finely sliced
1	head of pak choi, thinly sliced across
1	long red pepper, core and seeds removed, and sliced into thin strips 5–7cm long
¼	cucumber, thinly sliced diagonally
5	tablespoons coarsely chopped coriander, plus extra to serve
2	spring onions, trimmed and finely sliced

Dressing

2	tablespoons rice wine vinegar
1	teaspoon caster sugar
	pinch of sea salt
2	tablespoons sweet chilli sauce (hot)
1	tablespoon fish sauce (nam pla)
4	tablespoons groundnut oil

For the dressing, whisk the vinegar with the sugar and salt in a large bowl, then whisk in the remaining dressing ingredients. Fold in the prawns. Combine the Chinese leaves, pak choi, red pepper and cucumber in another large bowl. (You can prepare the salad to this point in advance, in which case cover and chill.)

Just before serving, toss the coriander into the prawns. Divide the salad between four plates or sundae glasses, spoon the prawns on top, drizzle over some of the dressing and scatter over the spring onions and a little more coriander. You can also assemble the ingredients in a jar or pot, or a lunchbox for instance. In this case, dress the prawns first then top with the salad to keep the leaves fresh.

ENERGY KCAL	CARBOHYDRATE G	SUGARS G	PROTEIN G	FAT G	SATURATED FAT G	SALT G
256	10.9	10.2	20.0	13.8	2.7	1.4

Crayfish, Rocket and Gherkins

Crayfish tends to get overlooked in favour of cold-water prawns, but its firm, meaty flesh lends itself to robust flavours and leaves. Here gherkins and rocket provide the attitude.

SERVES 2

Pot

100g	cooked and shelled crayfish tails
2	teaspoons lemon juice
3	teaspoons extra virgin olive oil
	black pepper
5cm	piece cucumber, peeled, quartered lengthways and thinly sliced
1	tablespoon finely sliced cocktail gherkins
2	handfuls of rocket, thickly sliced
1	teaspoon finely chopped chives
	Sesame Parmesan crackers (see page 21), optional

Dressing

1	rounded teaspoon mayonnaise
1	rounded teaspoon tomato ketchup
1	rounded tablespoon low-fat Greek yogurt

Dress the crayfish tails with the lemon juice and 2 teaspoons of olive oil in a small bowl and season with black pepper. For the dressing, blend the mayonnaise, ketchup and yogurt in another small bowl. Combine the cucumber, gherkins and remaining 1 teaspoon of olive oil in another small bowl.

Half-fill two small bowls or pots with rocket. Pile the cucumber mixture on top, then the crayfish, leaving behind any juices. Dollop the dressing on top of the crayfish and scatter over the chives. Serve with a couple of crackers, if wished. (The pots can be prepared a few hours in advance, in which case cover and chill).

ENERGY KCAL	CARBOHYDRATE G	SUGARS G	PROTEIN G	FAT G	SATURATED FAT G	SALT G
157	3.0	2.9	10.7	11.0	1.3	0.6

Ossau-Iraty, Roast Pepper, Buckwheat and Watercress

This pot has just enough buckwheat to be wholesome and take the edge off hunger without being heavy or stodgy. The unctuous maple syrup and mustard dressing is a real sparkler that ably partners the smooth, nutty cheese.

SERVES 2

Pot

4	tablespoons cooked buckwheat (30g uncooked*)
2	handfuls of watercress, coarsely chopped
2	heaped tablespoons finely sliced roast red peppers
30g	hard sheep's cheese (e.g. Ossau-Iraty), thinly sliced or shaved
2	tablespoons coarsely chopped flat-leaf parsley

Dressing

1	teaspoon grainy mustard
1	teaspoon maple syrup
1	teaspoon cider vinegar
	sea salt
2	tablespoons extra virgin olive oil

For the dressing, whisk the mustard, syrup, vinegar and a little salt together in a small bowl, then whisk in the oil.

For the pot, divide the buckwheat between two small bowls or pots and top with the watercress. Scatter over the pepper strips, then the cheese and the parsley. (The pots and dressing can be prepared a few hours in advance, in which case cover and chill.) Re-whisk the dressing and drizzle over the pots to serve.

Cook buckwheat in a pan of boiling salted water for 15 minutes until al dente, then drain into a sieve and leave to cool over the pan.

ENERGY KCAL	CARBOHYDRATE G	SUGARS G	PROTEIN G	FAT G	SATURATED FAT G	SALT G
267	15.7	3.6	6.1	19.5	6.1	0.6

Chicken, Avocado and Chilli Pot with Miso Dressing

This one is a personal favourite, and if you happen to be feeling particularly hungry, then I can recommend the addition of some edamame or black soya bean noodles into the line up.

Miso, with its natural umami, is made for salad dressings; satisfyingly punchy and particularly delicious with fresh ginger. If you have a good local health food store, then a fresh unpasteurised miso is the ideal – a world apart from the convenience jars. Given its shelf life, it is definitely worth a pilgrimage now and again.

SERVES 2

Pot

125g	cold roast chicken, shredded
1	small avocado, halved and stoned
	couple of squeezes of lime juice
	sea salt
2	handfuls of pea shoots, coarsely chopped
1	heaped tablespoon pine nuts
1	scant teaspoon very finely sliced medium-hot red chilli
2	teaspoons finely sliced spring onion

Dressing

½	teaspoon finely grated fresh ginger
1	heaped teaspoon brown miso (e.g. barley or rice)
1	teaspoon sherry vinegar
1	tablespoon groundnut oil
1	tablespoon water

Whisk together all the ingredients for the dressing in a medium bowl. Stir in the chicken and toss to coat.

Divide the chicken between two small bowls or pots. Slice each avocado half in its skin diagonally into thin strips. Scoop these out of the skin in one piece, fan them slightly on a plate, squeeze over some lime juice and season with a little salt. Transfer them, using a spatula, on top of the chicken. Pile the pea shoots in a layer on top of the avocado. Scatter over the pine nuts, then place a small pile of chilli and spring onion in the centre. (The pots can be prepared a few hours in advance, in which case cover and chill.) Toss to serve.

ENERGY KCAL	CARBOHYDRATE G	SUGARS G	PROTEIN G	FAT G	SATURATED FAT G	SALT G
357	3.2	1.5	23.7	26.7	4.5	0.8

Parma Ham with Figs and Sherried Stilton

Sherrying Stilton has long been my favourite ruse for the slightly hard and crumbly parts of the cheese that line the rind – a trickle of port is equally good. It is one of those secret indulgences like the dark and creamy 'oysters', the bits that sit just below the thighs on a roast chicken that are a choice titbit that deserves a cult of its own. So that's the excuse, with a few bits and bobs that serve to make it even more of a treat.

SERVES 4

1	tablespoon fino (dry) sherry
100g	Stilton, coarsely crumbled
1	head each red and green chicory, inner leaves
4	pickled walnuts, halved
2	fresh figs, stalks trimmed, cut into thin wedges
4	slices Parma ham

Pour the sherry over the Stilton in a medium bowl and gently work until just mixed in, without mashing it to a purée; there should still be little nibs of Stilton.

Lean a few mixed chicory leaves at the side of four small bowls, place a spoonful of the sherried cheese to one side, add a couple of walnut halves and a few fig wedges to each, then drape a slice of Parma ham to the side.

ENERGY KCAL	CARBOHYDRATE G	SUGARS G	PROTEIN G	FAT G	SATURATED FAT G	SALT G
193	3.3	3.1	11.8	14.0	6.9	1.4

Bresaola with Olives and Mozzarella

An oldie but a goodie, few of us can fail to find some kind of reassurance in a slice of Parma ham or bresaola served with soft skeins of mozzarella and tomato. The importance is the quality, something which we all know to our detriment if we have spent any amount of time hanging around airports waiting for delayed flights, when this is often the only salad on call. But if the destination is Italy, then all is well at the other end.

SERVES 2

Pot

2	handfuls of baby spinach or ruby chard leaves
10	pitted green olives, halved
6	baby mozzarellas
4	slices bresaola (air-cured beef) or Parma ham

Dressing

4	cherry tomatoes, finely chopped
	sea salt
1	teaspoon balsamic vinegar
1	tablespoon extra virgin olive oil
1	teaspoon finely chopped shallot

For the dressing, sprinkle the tomatoes with a little salt in a small bowl and set aside for 15 minutes. Add the balsamic vinegar, oil and shallot and stir.

Half-fill two small bowls or pots with spinach or ruby chard. Scatter over the olives and the mozzarellas. Drape the bresaola or Parma Ham in piles. (The pots and dressing can be prepared a few hours in advance, in which case cover and chill.) Spoon over the dressing to serve.

ENERGY KCAL	CARBOHYDRATE G	SUGARS G	PROTEIN G	FAT G	SATURATED FAT G	SALT G
206	1.8	1.7	10.9	16.7	6.4	1.5

Skinny Protein

This chapter is about the kind of suppers that I turn to several times a week when it is just the two of us, or maybe three or four, at the end of a busy day. The secret to a low-carb diet lies in having a little protein; it doesn't have to be a huge amount, just a small piece will make the difference to feeling sustained for the evening, and wards off those midnight snack attacks. And lots of veggies on the side; the only thing that stops me from having three or even four to choose from at the table is the time taken to prepare them, but certainly two is a must. So it's meat and two veg if you like, a combination that has stood the test of time even though we might endlessly reinvent and reshape the idea. These recipes would also be good for a decent lunch.

With the time constraints in mind, the ideal means to an end is flash-frying or griddling, which means that the cut of choice needs to be tender. So chicken breasts and thighs, lamb steaks and chops, pork fillet, and fish fillets such as salmon, sea bass and sea bream are the way to go, rather than slow-cooking casserole cuts that require hours to tenderise.

Thai Sea Bream Curry

There is something about curries with coconut that soothes at the same time as excites, and this soupy Thai bowl does just that. Like a fish soup, it will lend itself to the comparative austerity of just one tasty fish, as well as a selection. Sea bream is a personal favourite, but it could be worth scouring the freezer section for a fish pie mix that is diced and ready. Konjac noodles work well with these Asian flavours, as do edamame bean noodles.

SERVES 4

2	tablespoons vegetable oil
2	banana shallots, peeled, halved and thinly sliced
1	heaped tablespoon green or yellow Thai curry paste
1 x 400ml	can coconut milk (e.g. reduced fat)
1½	tablespoons lime juice
1	tablespoon fish sauce (nam pla)
1	heaped teaspoon palm or caster sugar
	sea salt
600g	sea bream fillets, skin on, cut into 3–5cm pieces
	handful of small basil leaves
	handful of coriander leaves
1	medium-hot green chilli, seeds removed and cut into long thin strips

Heat the oil in a large saucepan over a medium heat and fry the shallots for a few minutes until lightly coloured, stirring frequently. Stir in the curry paste and fry for about a minute, then add the coconut milk, lime juice, fish sauce, sugar and a little salt. Bring to the boil and simmer over a low heat for a few minutes, then season with a little more salt and add the fish, bring back to a simmer, cover and cook for a further 3–4 minutes.

Stir in half the basil and coriander leaves and taste to check the seasoning. Serve with the remaining herbs and chilli scattered over.

ENERGY KCAL	CARBOHYDRATE G	SUGARS G	PROTEIN G	FAT G	SATURATED FAT G	SALT G
312	5.1	4.0	28.1	19.4	6.7	1.7

Butter and Lemon Prawns with Spinach

Shell-on prawns gently simmered in butter provide a double treat – the tender meat within and sucking the bisque-scented juices from the shell. I have taken to rummaging around the freezer section for these, given that most shell-on prawns at the fish counter will have been frozen in any case, so why not ensure they are as fresh as possible? Allow a little extra for the water content once they are defrosted. This is very much a supper for two, which is all that will fit into a large frying pan.

SERVES 2

200g	spinach leaves, washed*
25g	unsalted butter
2	tablespoons extra virgin olive oil
1	garlic clove, peeled and crushed to a paste
350g	shell-on raw tiger prawns
	sea salt, black pepper
	juice of ½ lemon
	a small handful of coarsely chopped flat-leaf parsley

Put the washed spinach in a large saucepan, cover and steam over a gentle heat for 10 minutes until it collapses, stirring halfway through. Drain into a sieve or colander and press out the excess liquid using a potato masher.

Halfway through this time, heat a large, non-stick frying pan over a medium-high heat, add the butter and a tablespoon of oil and, once the butter has melted, stir in the garlic. Add the prawns, season and fry for 1½ minutes on each side until a dusty pink. Remove the pan from the heat, and transfer the prawns to a bowl. Add the lemon juice to the pan juices with the remaining tablespoon of oil, and stir in the parsley and a little seasoning. Return the prawns to the pan and stir to coat them. Serve beside the spinach, drizzling any juices in the pan over the vegetables.

Even if the spinach advertises it has been washed, pass the leaves under a cold tap in a colander – the water that clings to the leaves results in it steaming.

ENERGY KCAL	CARBOHYDRATE G	SUGARS G	PROTEIN G	FAT G	SATURATED FAT G	SALT G
398	2.2	1.8	38.4	25.1	8.8	1.5

One-pot Fillet-o-fish with Spinach and Nutmeg

An idle stroll across our local green to the indoor market on the other side offers the reward of a vegetable shop that is a treasure-trove of exotica and verdant greens sold by the glossy bunch. The spinach comes as though freshly tugged from the ground, roots, stalks and all, which are as thick as your thumb and give the vegetable a depth of flavour like some lost memory. The kind of seasonal produce that has us religiously making tracks to a farmers' market.

Hake is a meaty white fish that may not attract as much attention as the staples but is every bit as characterful, in fact more so than cod. My preference is to cook the fish as one big fillet to ensure the flesh remains especially succulent. This also lends itself to a garlicky mayonnaise and some capers, grand aioli-style.

SERVES 2

400g	spinach, washed*
3	tablespoons extra virgin olive oil
2	fat spring onions, trimmed and thinly sliced
125g	chestnut or wild mushrooms, trimmed and sliced or torn
	freshly grated nutmeg
	sea salt, black pepper
150g	cherry tomatoes, halved
250–300g	skinned hake fillet
	coarsely chopped flat-leaf parsley

TO SERVE

2	heaped teaspoons garlic mayonnaise
2	heaped teaspoons small (non-pareil) capers, rinsed

Put the washed spinach in a large saucepan, cover and steam over a gentle heat for 10 minutes until it collapses, stirring halfway through. Drain into a sieve or colander and press out the excess liquid using a potato masher.

Heat the olive oil in the same saucepan over a medium-low heat and fry the spring onions for a couple of minutes until softened, stirring frequently. Add the mushrooms, and continue to fry for a further couple of minutes until these too soften, stirring now and again. Should any liquid be given out, continue to cook until this evaporates. Stir in the spinach and season with nutmeg, salt and pepper and heat through. Stir in the tomatoes, lay the fish on top and season, then cover the pan and cook over a low heat for 5–10 minutes (depending on whether you are cooking individual fillets or one large one), until the fish has lost its translucency. Serve scattered with parsley, accompanied by mayonnaise and capers.

*See opposite page.

ENERGY KCAL	CARBOHYDRATE G	SUGARS G	PROTEIN G	FAT G	SATURATED FAT G	SALT G
342	33.2	6.4	33.2	17.8	2.5	1.3

Crispy Salmon with Green Bean Mimosa

This method of cooking salmon fillets in their own oil, which ensures they emerge from the pan crisp to the point of brittle at the edges while the centre remains succulent and buttery, is on a loop in our house and I have to fight my corner if I cook it any other way. A smattering of finely chopped egg provides a little delicacy.

SERVES 4

4	medium eggs
500g	fine French beans, stalk ends trimmed
25g	salted butter
½	teaspoon finely grated lemon zest, plus a generous squeeze of juice
4	tablespoons coarsely chopped flat-leaf parsley
	sea salt, black pepper
4x 150g	skinned salmon fillets*

Thirty minutes in advance of eating, bring a small pan of water to the boil, add the eggs and cook for 10 minutes, then drain, refill the pan with cold water and leave to cool. Separate out the whites and yolks, discard two of the whites and finely chop the remaining two and also the yolks, then combine them.

The beans and salmon can be cooked about 10 minutes in advance of eating. Bring a large pan of salted water to the boil, add the beans and cook for 3–4 minutes until just tender. Drain into a colander and leave to steam-dry for a few minutes. Gently melt the butter in the pan, then return the beans, scatter over the lemon zest, add a squeeze of juice and gently toss, and mix in half the parsley.

To cook the salmon, heat a large non-stick frying pan over a medium heat, season and fry the top side for about 5 minutes until golden and crispy and you can see that it has cooked through by a third to half, then turn and cook the other side for about 3 minutes – exact timings will depend on the thickness of the fillet, it should have just lost its translucency in the centre.

Serve the salmon on top of the beans, scatter over the egg mimosa and remaining parsley.

*The salmon should give out enough oil during the first few minutes of frying to crisp the flesh, but just occasionally you might find you need to add a drop of oil to the pan.

ENERGY KCAL	CARBOHYDRATE G	SUGARS G	PROTEIN G	FAT G	SATURATED FAT G	SALT G
469	4.0	2.8	44.0	29.6	8.0	0.4

Teriyaki Salmon with Baby Kale Salad and Coconut Dressing

This voluptuous coconut dressing has the texture of salad cream, and will stand in for all manner of occasions. Especially good drizzled over baby kale, our favourite new leaf on the block.

SERVES 4

650g	skinned salmon fillet
2	tablespoons teriyaki marinade (e.g. Kikkoman)
1	tablespoon coconut oil
1	bunch (6–8) spring onions, trimmed and finely sliced
100g	baby kale or baby spinach
1	medium-hot red chilli, core and seeds discarded, cut into fine strips 2–3cm long

Dressing

3	rounded tablespoons coconut yogurt
2	tablespoons coconut cream or milk
2	teaspoons dark soy sauce
1	teaspoon lime juice
1	rounded teaspoon palm or caster sugar

Cut off the thin belly section to one side of the salmon fillet and reserve this for another use. Slice the remaining fillet across into strips 1–2cm thick. Pour the marinade over the salmon in a large bowl, stirring to coat it. (Cover and chill for up to half a day.)

Whisk all the ingredients for the dressing together in a small bowl – it should be a thick pouring consistency. (Cover and chill until required.)

Heat the coconut oil in a large, non-stick frying pan over a medium heat and fry the spring onions for 6–10 minutes until golden, stirring frequently. Heat a second large, non-stick frying pan over a medium-high heat and fry the salmon strips in batches for about 1 minute on the first side and 30 seconds on the second, carefully turning them using a spatula. There is no need to add any oil to the pan, and the fish should colour and caramelise almost instantly. Reserve the salmon on a warm plate.

Arrange a pile of leaves with a few strips of chilli on four serving plates and spoon over a little of the dressing. Place the salmon to the side, and scatter the spring onions over the strips.

ENERGY KCAL	CARBOHYDRATE G	SUGARS G	PROTEIN G	FAT G	SATURATED FAT G	SALT G
401	3.6	3.1	36.3	26.5	9.8	1.1

Scallop Tikka

Ready-prepped scallop meats make this the quickest of suppers. But then again, if they do come with the corals, so often discarded but something I have a secret crush on, then these can also be included. Something bread-like for mopping is good here, the Coconut Almond Bread (see page 18) and a veggie on the side would be ideal.

SERVES 4

400g	scallop meats, side gristle discarded
100g	frozen petits pois
	sea salt

Marinade

2	tablespoons vegetable oil
1	shallot, peeled and finely chopped
2	garlic cloves, peeled and finely chopped
1	teaspoon finely chopped fresh ginger
1	teaspoon finely chopped medium-hot red chilli
⅓	teaspoon ground turmeric
¼	teaspoon ground cinnamon
½	teaspoon ground fenugreek
100g	low-fat yogurt
½	teaspoon cornflour

TO SERVE

2	spring onions, trimmed and finely sliced diagonally
	small handful of coriander leaves
	lime wedges

For the marinade, heat a tablespoon of vegetable oil in a small non-stick frying pan over a medium heat and fry the shallot, garlic, ginger and chilli for a couple of minutes until softened, stirring frequently, then stir in the spices and cook for a little longer until fragrant. Transfer this to a food processor and leave for a few minutes to cool, then add the yogurt and cornflour and whizz to a purée. Transfer this to a bowl and stir in the scallops. (You can leave them to marinate for up to a couple of hours, in which case cover and chill them.)

Preheat the oven to 220°C fan/240°C electric/gas mark 9. Stir the petit pois into the scallops and season with salt, and spread over the base of a roasting pan. Drizzle over the remaining tablespoon of oil and roast for 9–12 minutes until the scallops are just cooked through; they should feel firm with a slight give.

Combine the spring onions and coriander leaves in a bowl and serve scattered over the scallop tikka, accompanied by lime wedges.

ENERGY KCAL	CARBOHYDRATE G	SUGARS G	PROTEIN G	FAT G	SATURATED FAT G	SALT G
201	5.5	3.5	26.1	7.9	1.0	0.5

Mackerel, Chicory and Apple Roast

Roasting mackerel in the oven transforms this humble fish – it is my favourite way of cooking it – and that essential oiliness comes up a treat with a sharp mustard dressing, apples and chicory.

SERVES 6

6	heads of Belgian chicory, trimmed and separated into leaves
2	eating apples, peeled, quartered, cored and thinly sliced
approx. 7	tablespoons extra virgin olive oil
	sea salt, black pepper
1	teaspoon Dijon mustard
1	teaspoon grainy mustard
1	tablespoon cider vinegar
1	tablespoon finely chopped walnuts
approx. 600g	fresh mackerel fillets
	flat-leaf parsley, to serve

Preheat the oven to 220°C fan /240°C electric/gas mark 9. Place the chicory leaves and apple slices in a large roasting pan (e.g. 25 x 35cm) with 3 tablespoons of olive oil to coat them and season with salt. Roast for 15 minutes, stirring halfway through.

Meanwhile, whisk the mustards with the vinegar and some seasoning in a small bowl, then whisk in 3 tablespoons of oil, one at a time, and add the walnuts.

Also heat a large, non-stick frying pan over a high heat. Brush the mackerel fillets on each side with the remaining oil and season them, then sear the skin for 1 minute; you will need to do this in batches, carefully removing them with a spatula.

Lay the mackerel fillets, skin-side up, on top of the chicory and apple, drizzle over the dressing and return to the oven for 5 minutes. Serve scattered with parsley.

ENERGY KCAL	CARBOHYDRATE G	SUGARS G	PROTEIN G	FAT G	SATURATED FAT G	SALT G
483	7.5	7.3	21.6	40.0	7.7	0.6

Spicy Fried Chicken

These spicy fried chicken strips cut to the quick for this genre of food, slightly crisp with a spicy coating. You might consider the centre of a young lettuce leaf with a splodge of mayo or guacamole (see page 42 or 128) if they haven't proved too hard to resist nibbling on their own. And if they should make it, then a simple sliced tomato salad will raise the healthy bar even higher.

SERVES 2

300g	skinless free-range chicken fillets (approx. 2)
1	teaspoon turmeric
1	teaspoon ground cumin
1	teaspoon ground coriander
1	teaspoon cayenne pepper
2	tablespoons sesame seeds
1	tablespoon ground almonds
	sea salt
	groundnut or vegetable oil for shallow-frying

TO SERVE

coarsely chopped coriander

lemon wedges

Cut out any visible white tendon from the underside of the chicken fillets and gently bash them with a rolling pin to flatten slightly. Slice the fillets across into strips about 1.5cm thick. Combine the spices, sesame seeds and almonds in a wide shallow bowl. Dab the chicken strips with water either side, and season with salt, then dip them a few at a time either side into the spice mixture, pressing down so the sesame seeds stick. You will probably only use about half the mixture. Set aside on a plate.

Heat about 5mm of oil in a large non-stick frying pan over a medium heat for a few minutes until a piece of chicken sizzles when submerged. Fry them half at a time, for approximately 1½ minutes on the first side and 1 minute on the second, then drain on a double thickness of kitchen paper while you cook the remainder. Transfer to a plate, scatter with coriander and accompany with lemon wedges.

ENERGY KCAL	CARBOHYDRATE G	SUGARS G	PROTEIN G	FAT G	SATURATED FAT G	SALT G
348	2.0	0.5	40.0	19.2	3.3	0.2

Chicken and Coconut Balti

Don't be daunted by the slightly lengthy list of aromatics, having whizzed around the kitchen gathering them up you are still only 30 minutes away from a delectably soupy and fragrant curry. I would serve this with a mixture of whole grains and vegetables such as courgettes or leeks, and something leafy like rocket.

SERVES 4

2	garlic cloves, peeled
1 x 4cm	knob of fresh ginger, peeled
1	teaspoon chopped medium-hot red chilli
2	tablespoons groundnut or vegetable oil
1	large onion, peeled and finely chopped
1	cinnamon stick
6	green cardamom pods
6	cloves
6	curry leaves
1	tablespoon garam masala
1	teaspoon ground turmeric
1	heaped teaspoon tamarind paste
4	tomatoes*, cores cut out, and coarsely chopped
600g	skinless free-range chicken fillets, cut into 2–3cm dice
	sea salt
1 x 400ml	can full-fat coconut milk**

Whizz the garlic, ginger and chilli to a coarse paste in a food processor. Heat the oil in a large saucepan over a low heat and fry the onion with the cinnamon stick, cardamom, cloves and curry leaves for about 10 minutes until golden, stirring frequently. Stir in the garlic mixture and fry for a minute longer.

Meanwhile, blend the garam masala, tumeric and tamarind with 2 tablespoons of water in a small bowl. Stir this into the onion and cook briefly until fragrant. Add the tomatoes and cook for a couple of minutes longer until mushy, stirring frequently.

Add the chicken to the curry base, give it a good stir and season with salt, then cover and cook over a low heat for 10 minutes, stirring a couple of times, until it is just cooked through. Stir the thick bank of coconut cream at the top of the can into the curry, leaving behind the coconut water that can be reserved for some other use. Heat through without boiling, then serve.

If you want to skin the tomatoes, knick the bases with a sharp knife, then plunge them first into boiling water for about 20 seconds and then into a bowl of cold water until cool enough to handle.

**Providing the can hasn't been shaken or turned, the cream will have settled at the top.*

ENERGY KCAL	CARBOHYDRATE G	SUGARS G	PROTEIN G	FAT G	SATURATED FAT G	SALT G
363	11.2	9.2	38.2	17.1	8.8	0.3

Creamy Saffron Chicken and Celeriac Salad

A classic style of salad that has a certain old-world glamour despite celeriac standing in for potato – just as good. And of the type that is just right for a relaxed lunch in the garden with friends. This one will be good for a couple of days, so it is worth making up a generous quantity.

There are a couple of time-saving tips if you want to speed the process. First is to boil the water for cooking the celeriac in a kettle, and second is to spread it out on a tray once it is cooked, to cool quickly. As for the cooked chicken, this is a good excuse to roast up a nice juicy bird even if there are only two of you, and the cold meat can be used for this salad in the days that follow. Equally it is extremely good made with guinea fowl – an average-sized bird should provide just enough meat. Some small caper berries might also be good for scattering over at the end instead of the extra capers.

SERVES 6

	slug of white wine vinegar or cider vinegar
750g	celeriac, peeled and cut into 2cm dice
	small pinch of saffron filaments (approx. 10)
150ml	soured cream
150ml	0%-fat Greek yogurt
1	heaped teaspoon grainy mustard
	sea salt, black pepper
2	tablespoons finely chopped shallots
2	tablespoons small (non-pareil) capers, rinsed, plus extra to serve
500g	cooked chicken, cut into strips 5–7cm long
30g	roast Marcona almonds, or coarsely chopped roast almonds
	chopped chervil or flat-leaf parsley, §to serve

Bring a large pan of salted water to the boil and acidulate it with a slug of vinegar. Add the celeriac and cook for about 7 minutes or until tender. Drain into a colander, run under the cold tap and then set aside for about 10 minutes to cool to ambient temperature.

Grind the saffron filaments using a pestle and mortar, then add a teaspoon of boiling water. Blend the soured cream, yogurt, saffron infusion, mustard and plenty of seasoning in a large bowl, then mix in the shallots and capers. Add the celeriac and coat in the dressing, then loosely mix in the chicken; it doesn't have to be thoroughly coated.

Spread this out on a serving dish, then scatter over the almonds, a few extra capers, and some chervil or parsley. (It can be prepared well in advance, in which case cover and chill, and bring back up to room temperature to serve.)

ENERGY KCAL	CARBOHYDRATE G	SUGARS G	PROTEIN G	FAT G	SATURATED FAT G	SALT G
255	4.2	3.6	32.4	11.2	4.5	0.7

Lamb Steaks with Mint Sauce and Feta

Lamb with mint sauce will ever evoke memories of family Sunday lunches, but here some roast peppers and feta give it a new lease of life.

You can always cheat with a jar of ready-made peppers, but otherwise it only takes a minute or two to prepare a tray for the oven, especially now that we have baby ones to call on that don't require any chopping.

SERVES 6

600g	lamb steaks (leg or chump), 2–3cm thick
150g	feta, coarsely crumbled
200g	mini roast peppers or strips*

Mint Sauce

25g	mint leaves
4	tablespoons extra virgin olive oil, plus extra for frying
2	teaspoons red wine vinegar
½	teaspoon caster sugar
	sea salt, black pepper

For the mint sauce, put the mint, oil, vinegar, sugar and a little salt in a food processor and whizz to a fine purée, then taste and add a little more salt, if necessary.

Heat a teaspoon of oil in a large non-stick frying pan over a high heat. Season the lamb steaks on each side and fry for 5–6 minutes in total until golden; a slight give to them without being too squashy will indicate they are medium-rare. Remove to a warm plate to rest for a few minutes.

Arrange the lamb on plates, scatter with feta, spoon over a generous teaspoon of the sauce and place the peppers on top. To serve, cut off the fat and thinly slice the steaks.

*Cut the top off 400g mini peppers and nick out the seeds inside. Arrange in a crowded layer in a roasting pan, drizzle over a couple of tablespoons of extra virgin olive oil, season and roast for about 40 minutes at 190°C fan/210°C electric/gas mark 6½ until golden, turning them halfway through. Leave to cool.

ENERGY KCAL	CARBOHYDRATE G	SUGARS G	PROTEIN G	FAT G	SATURATED FAT G	SALT G
333	3.8	3.5	23.8	24.6	9.8	0.9

Lamb Steaks with Broccoli Mash

Lamb steaks such as leg or chump are as tender as fillet, and carry the same convenience as chops, while a rustic broccoli mash stands in lieu of potatoes. The two together are smothered in a tasty little sauce with pine nuts and sun-dried tomatoes.

SERVES 4

2	tablespoons extra virgin olive oil
	sea salt, black pepper
4	lamb steaks (leg or chump, approx 150g each), 2–3cm thick
600g	broccoli florets
15g	salted butter
25g	pine nuts
2	tablespoons oregano or marjoram leaves, or 2 teaspoons coarsely chopped rosemary needles
1	tablespoon balsamic vinegar
4	sun-dried tomato halves, sliced
1	teaspoon pink peppercorns, finely chopped (optional)

Bring a large pan of salted water to the boil. Heat a tablespoon of oil in a large non-stick frying pan over a medium heat, season the lamb steaks either side and fry for about 5 minutes in total until golden; a slight give to them without being too squashy will indicate they are medium-rare. Then turn them on their sides to colour the fat, and remove to a warm plate to rest for a few minutes.

Having put the steaks on, boil the broccoli for about 6 minutes until tender, then drain it into a colander and leave for a few minutes to steam-dry. Whizz to a textured purée in a food processor with the butter and some seasoning.

Drain the fat off the frying pan, add a tablespoon of oil to the pan and fry the pine nuts and herbs until lightly golden, stirring frequently, then add the balsamic vinegar and sizzle to reduce by half. Remove from the heat and stir in the sun-dried tomatoes, which should warm through. Serve this spooned over the lamb steaks and broccoli mash, with a little pink pepper scattered over, if wished.

ENERGY KCAL	CARBOHYDRATE G	SUGARS G	PROTEIN G	FAT G	SATURATED FAT G	SALT G
490	5.2	4.3	50.0	28.2	10.4	0.4

Lamb Chops with Coriander, Ginger and Chilli

I have always found marinades a bit of a muddle, and prefer just a few sharp flavours. This kind of simple fresh marinade is my staple when grilling chops and fillets, it adds in a little pizzazz without recourse to lengthy steeping. So you could use this for any small cut you are frying up.

SERVES 4

4	tablespoons extra virgin olive oil, plus extra for the leaves
	finely grated zest of 1 lemon, plus a generous tablespoon of juice, plus a squeeze for the salad
3	garlic cloves, peeled and crushed to a paste
1	tablespoon finely grated fresh ginger
1	heaped teaspoon finely chopped medium-hot red chilli
1	teaspoon ground coriander
4	lamb loin chops (approx. 150–180g each)
	sea salt, black pepper
	coarsely chopped coriander
	baby salad leaves, to serve
½	avocado, stoned, skinned and cut into thin slivers

Make a marinade with the olive oil, lemon zest and juice, garlic, ginger, chilli and ground coriander in a large bowl. Add the lamb chops and coat them in the mixture. (You can do this up to a couple of hours before eating, in which case cover and chill.)

Heat a large non-stick frying pan over a medium-high heat. Season the chops either side and fry them for about 4 minutes on each side to leave them pink in the centre – they should have a slight give when pressed without feeling soft – then stand them on their sides to colour the fat. Leave these to rest for a few minutes in a warm serving dish. Drain off the fat, add any leftover marinade to the pan and allow it to sizzle off the heat for about 30 seconds, then spoon this over the chops and scatter over some chopped coriander.

Serve with a little salad dressed with olive oil to coat the leaves, a squeeze of lemon and pinch of salt, and some slivers of avocado.

ENERGY KCAL	CARBOHYDRATE G	SUGARS G	PROTEIN G	FAT G	SATURATED FAT G	SALT G
514	0.6	0.4	34.3	41.0	18.0	0.3

Bavette Steak with Courgette Mash and Olives

Bavette *and* onglet *steaks (and* hampe, *should you be in France) are characterised by their long and tender fibres; fab cuts that are popular bistro and gastro pub fare. They should always be cooked rare or medium-rare to remain tender. Two is the perfect number for a steak supper, and with literally a couple of minutes grilling here, these fall into the 'minute' steak genre. The mash mirrors that ease, deliciously sweet and offset by the salty olives. Be sure to give the meat 30 minutes at room temperature before cooking, otherwise the fibres may toughen.*

SERVES 2

1	tablespoon extra virgin olive oil, plus extra for brushing the steaks
10g	unsalted butter
500g	courgettes, ends discarded, and sliced
1	tablespoon lemon juice
	sea salt, black pepper
2	onglet or bavette steaks (approx. 125–150g each), 1–1.5cm thick*
2	teaspoons grainy mustard
30g	pitted green olives, coarsely chopped

Heat a tablespoon of oil and the butter in a large saucepan over a medium heat and fry the courgettes for about 5 minutes until glossy and starting to colour, stirring frequently. Season them, cover the pan, and cook over a low heat for 5 minutes until soft and golden on the base. Whizz the contents of the pan to a purée with the lemon juice in a food processor. (This can be made in advance, chilled in the fridge and gently reheated in a small, non-stick saucepan before serving.)

Having put the courgettes on to cook, heat a ridged griddle over a high heat for several minutes. Brush the steaks with oil and season on each side, then grill for 1 minute on the first side and 45–60 seconds on the second, pressing down with a spatula to help brand the steaks with stripes. They should have a slight give when pressed without feeling squashy, to leave them medium-rare. Transfer them to a warm plate and cover with foil to keep warm while they rest for 5–10 minutes.

Smear the steaks with the mustard, and serve with the courgette mash, scattered with chopped olives.

If your steaks are any thicker than this, pound them using a rolling pin.

ENERGY KCAL	CARBOHYDRATE G	SUGARS G	PROTEIN G	FAT G	SATURATED FAT G	SALT G
357	5.1	4.8	36.1	19.9	6.7	1.2

Paprika Pork with Chicory and Lemon

Pork fillet is one of my go-to cuts for a fast supper; lean and tender – be sure to leave it with a tinge of blush pink in the centre. As fillet goes, it is kinder on the pocket than either beef or lamb, so you are more likely to turn to pork as a matter of course. And you can serve the medallions cooked this way with any vegetable of your choice, although the chicory is especially good.

SERVES 4

1 x 450g	pork fillet, sliced into medallions 2cm thick
1	tablespoon extra virgin olive oil, plus extra for brushing the pork
	sea salt
	hot paprika
10g	unsalted butter
500g	Belgian chicory, base trimmed and very thinly sliced across
1	tablespoon lemon juice
1	teaspoon cornflour blended with 1 teaspoon water
1	heaped teaspoon grainy mustard
30g	soured cream
	handful of finely chopped flat-leaf parsley, plus extra to serve

Brush the pork medallions with oil, and lightly season either side with salt and paprika. Heat a large non-stick frying pan over a medium heat for several minutes and fry half the medallions at a time for about 2 minutes on each side until golden. They should feel firm when pressed, with a slight give, and a hint of pink when you cut into them. Set aside on a warm plate to rest for 5 minutes.

While the pork is cooking, heat a tablespoon of oil and the butter in a medium-large saucepan over a low heat. Add the chicory and stir to coat, then season with salt and add the lemon juice. Cover and cook for 10 minutes, stirring halfway through. Add the cornflour mixture and stir for about a minute, then stir in the mustard, soured cream and parsley.

Serve the chicory with the pork medallions, scattering over some extra parsley.

ENERGY KCAL	CARBOHYDRATE G	SUGARS G	PROTEIN G	FAT G	SATURATED FAT G	SALT G
285	2.6	1.4	39.2	12.7	4.8	0.3

Salami, Grilled Sprouting Broccoli and Figs

Blanching purple sprouting broccoli before popping it onto a hot griddle to sear has to be one of the finest treatments for this northerly vegetable, one that remains a seasonal treat and trumps long-stem broccoli for both sweetness and its leafy greens. Any cured hams can be dished up alongside, and the dried figs and pickled walnuts round the assembly off to a tee.

SERVES 6

500g	purple sprouting broccoli
approx. 4	tablespoons extra virgin olive oil
	sea salt, black pepper
2	bunches of slim spring onions (6–8 per bunch), trimmed
12	slices each of pastrami and German salami
6	dried figs, stalks trimmed, halved downwards
9	pickled walnuts, halved downwards

Bring a large pan of salted water to the boil. Trim the base of the broccoli stalks where they appear to become tough, so they are about 12cm long, and then peel the last few centimetres or tips of the stalks. Add the broccoli to the boiling water, pushing it well down, and cook for 3 minutes, then drain into a colander and shake dry.

Heat a griddle over a medium heat. Toss the broccoli in a large bowl with oil to coat it and season, and likewise the spring onions in another large bowl. Grill the broccoli in batches for about 2 minutes on each side until patched with gold, and then repeat with the spring onions, arranging them together to one side of a large serving plate as you go. They can be eaten hot or cold.

Arrange the pastrami and salami with the figs and walnuts to the side of the vegetables.

ENERGY KCAL	CARBOHYDRATE G	SUGARS G	PROTEIN G	FAT G	SATURATED FAT G	SALT G
246	14.3	14.0	11.4	14.4	3.0	0.9

Basil Burgers with Tzatziki

These burgers have the wow factor of a heady hit of basil, but you could vary this with, for instance, some mint, flat-leaf parsley and chives. Anything soft and fragrant that lends itself to being eaten in quantity. You can also use minced beef instead of lamb, so it's a good all-rounder to have up your sleeve.

SERVES 4

4	tomatoes, thinly sliced across, core/top slices discarded
8	small crisp lettuce leaves
100g	tzatziki

Burgers

50g	basil leaves
1	banana shallot, peeled and coarsely chopped
1	teaspoon sumac
1	garlic clove, peeled
1	tablespoon extra virgin olive oil
	sea salt, black pepper
500–600g	lean minced lamb

Put all the burger ingredients except the lamb in a food processor and reduce to a coarse purée. Blend this with the lamb in a large bowl and form into eight burgers, by shaping balls of the mixture the size of a clementine. For the neatest results, press them into a 9–10cm cutter. (These can be made well in advance, in which case cover and chill them.)

Heat a large non-stick frying pan over a medium heat and fry the burgers in batches for about 2 minutes on each side until golden and firm when pressed, draining the fat from the pan when necessary. Lay a couple of tomato slices in a lettuce leaf, season, then pop a couple of burgers on top and dollop with the tzatziki. Enclose with a second leaf.

ENERGY KCAL	CARBOHYDRATE G	SUGARS G	PROTEIN G	FAT G	SATURATED FAT G	SALT G
307	6.9	5.7	28.8	17.2	7.1	0.5

Very Veggie

We all know how easy it is to steam or blanch fresh seasonal offerings and toss them in butter or oil in a moment, and that simple treatment certainly fits the remit of this book – as do plain green salads and the like – but it is the more ambitious combinations that may not instantly spring to mind when you are thinking about lunch or dinner. These recipes are a celebration of the wonderful jazzy ensembles that vegetables lend themselves to, with less usual dressings relying on ingredients like miso, pomegranate syrup, yuzu, orange and sesame, that take them one step beyond the obvious. Most of these will serve you well as a light lunch, a starter, are good for grazing, or can be eked out with a little griddled chicken or cold meat as a main.

Cocktail Avos

The neat hole created by removing the stone from an avocado begs to be filled. And these mini avos have more panache than that one lonely retro half: three little tasters to choose from. These days avocados tend to come in small, medium and large. I find the small ones ideal for solo snacking, where a medium one can be too much, and the second half is not something to pop back into the fridge for posterity.

There is no need to make up all of the suggestions, unless there are two or more of you. Just one will do if you are alone. For a veggie option, you could replace the shrimps with chopped hard-boiled egg, leaving out the lemon juice.

SERVES 4

4	tablespoons extra virgin olive oil
	sea salt, black pepper
1	tablespoon balsamic vinegar
6	small avocados, halved and stoned

Pistachio

50g	pistachios
	sea salt
	cayenne pepper

Feta

50g	feta, crumbled
1	heaped teaspoon finely chopped mint
1	teaspoon lemon juice

Shrimp

50g	cooked and peeled brown shrimp
1	heaped teaspoon finely chopped flat-leaf parsley
1	teaspoon lemon juice

Whizz the pistachios in a food processor with a little salt and cayenne pepper for 4–5 minutes, until the crumbs are sticky and clinging together, but without turning into a paste. Combine the feta, mint, lemon juice and ½ tablespoon of olive oil in a small bowl. Combine the shrimps, parsley, lemon juice and ½ tablespoon of olive oil in another small bowl.

Whisk the balsamic vinegar with a little seasoning in a small bowl, then stir in the remaining 3 tablespoons of oil.

Divide the avocados between four plates so you have three halves on each one. If you like, you can nick a small slice off the base of each half so they stand level; this is most easily done before you halve and stone them. Pile the avocado holes with the pistachio, feta and shrimp fillings so you have one of each per plate. Drizzle the balsamic vinaigrette over all three and around the edges then serve.

ENERGY KCAL	CARBOHYDRATE G	SUGARS G	PROTEIN G	FAT G	SATURATED FAT G	SALT G
439	2.2	1.9	8.4	43.0	9.4	0.5

Salad of Endive with Chicken Livers

Chicken livers hide their light under a bushel – tasty, fast and affordable, and rich in iron as well as a host of other micronutrients. It is, however, sufficiently rare to encounter really good free-range ones so, when you do, it is worth stocking up on a few tubs and popping them in the freezer. The one proviso, which is all too easy to overlook, is to cook the livers through. Slightly pink in the centre is both fine and desirable, but never bloody, which carries the same risks as eating undercooked chicken.

In France, where gésiers (gizzards) and chicken livers are common currency in bistro salads, you can also buy packets of confit livers, preserved in duck fat ready to hit the pan, and already cooked. And these were the starting point for this salad with its mustardy dressing. This makes a little more dressing than you will need, but it keeps well for a couple of weeks in a screw-top jar in the fridge.

SERVES 3

200g	free-range chicken livers
1	large or 2 small heads of Belgian chicory, ends trimmed
50g	coarsely chopped walnuts
1	tablespoon duck or goose fat, or extra virgin olive oil
	small handful of coarsely chopped flat-leaf parsley

Dressing

1	rounded teaspoon Dijon mustard
	sea salt, black pepper
3	tablespoons groundnut oil
1	teaspoon red wine or cider vinegar

Start by making the dressing. Whisk the mustard with a little seasoning in a medium bowl, scrunching the salt if it is flaky. Whisk in the oil, a tablespoon at a time, until thick and mayonnaise-like. Stir in the vinegar and just enough water to thin the vinaigrette to the consistency of single cream, about 2 teaspoons.

Cut the chicken lobes off the tough central membranes that join them, and slice the livers into even pieces a few centimetres across. Halve the chicory heads lengthways, slice these into long thin strips and then halve across. Toss these in a large salad bowl with just enough dressing to coat the leaves, about half, and mix in the walnuts.

Heat the fat or oil in a large non-stick frying pan over a medium-high heat, add the chicken livers, season and fry for a couple of minutes, turning as they start to colour, until they are golden with a slight give to indicate they are medium-rare in the centre. Spoon these over the salad, scatter over the parsley and serve straight away.

ENERGY KCAL	CARBOHYDRATE G	SUGARS G	PROTEIN G	FAT G	SATURATED FAT G	SALT G
345	1.3	1.0	15.3	30.6	4.0	0.3

Courgette Noodle Salad with Smoked Salmon

There is no need for a spiraliser here, a trusted swivel-head vegetable peeler will do a fine job of reducing slim courgettes to a pile of pappardelle – otherwise-austere veggies do acquire a new-found glamour treated this way.

SERVES 4

1	tablespoon toasted sesame oil
6	garlic cloves, peeled and finely sliced
500g	slim courgettes, ends removed
6	radishes, trimmed and finely sliced across
2	tablespoons toasted sesame seeds
200g	smoked salmon, sliced across into strips 3–4cm wide
4	large pinches of mustard and cress, or alfalfa

Dressing

1	tablespoon yuzu juice
½	teaspoon finely grated orange zest
1	teaspoon caster sugar
	sea salt
1	tablespoon toasted sesame oil

To make the dressing, whisk the yuzu juice, orange zest, sugar and a little salt in a small bowl, then stir in the sesame oil.

Heat the oil in a medium, non-stick frying pan over a medium heat and briefly fry the garlic until lightly coloured, stirring frequently. Spread out on a double thickness of kitchen paper and leave to cool.

Using a potato peeler, turn the courgettes into long ribbons – you can keep the sections that are hard to peel for frying. Toss the ribbons and radishes with the dressing in a large bowl, then mix in the seeds. Divide between four plates. Pile the smoked salmon on top, then the cress and scatter over the garlic and serve.

ENERGY KCAL	CARBOHYDRATE G	SUGARS G	PROTEIN G	FAT G	SATURATED FAT G	SALT G
220	4.5	3.8	15.4	14.8	2.7	1.5

Seaweed Salad with Miso Dressing

A supper of tuna tataki on a bed of different coloured seaweeds eaten at a small restaurant in Mallorca was a revelation. Having encountered nori, wakami and other seaweeds, these frilly green, pink and ivory fronds were intriguing. I assumed they were the proceeds of artful foraging from the surrounding bays, but later encountered bags of kaiso mix in a local deli and they are, in fact, Japanese in origin. While a mild disappointment in terms of terroir, *the good news is you can find kaiso on Amazon.*

But going back to that tataki with its sticky sweet and salty dressing, a nice slab of lightly seared meaty fish – tuna, salmon, or grilled prawns or scallops – would be just the ticket with this salad, which is rich in texture and flavour. This is a tad more dressing than you might require, with plenty of uses thereafter.

SERVES 2

Salad

8g	dried kaiso mix seaweed
4	small tomatoes
	sea salt
¼	cucumber, peeled and very finely sliced
1	large or 2 small avocados, halved and stoned
1	teaspoon finely sliced medium-hot red chilli
2	teaspoons sesame seeds

Dressing

1	teaspoon finely grated fresh ginger
1	level tablespoon brown miso (e.g. barley or rice)
2	teaspoons sherry vinegar
2	tablespoons groundnut oil

Put the seaweed in a medium bowl, cover plentifully with cold water and soak for 20 minutes, then drain and spin dry in a salad spinner. Meanwhile, thinly slice the tomatoes, season with a little salt in a bowl and set aside for 15 minutes. Whisk all the ingredients for the dressing together, with 2 tablespoons of water, in a medium bowl.

Combine the tomatoes and cucumber on a large plate and mix in the seaweed. Slice the avocado into long, fine strips in the skin, then use a dessertspoon to remove the slices in one go and arrange these in a pile in the middle of the salad. Drizzle over the dressing and scatter with chilli and sesame seeds.

ENERGY KCAL	CARBOHYDRATE G	SUGARS G	PROTEIN G	FAT G	SATURATED FAT G	SALT G
188	6.6	5.6	2.7	14.9	1.3	0.7

Avocado and Green Bean Salad with Pomegranate Dressing

Avocado oil is unctuous and dense, the fruit in liquid form, and when you marry the two, it provides an extra dimension. In addition, it goes especially well with pomegranate syrup. I find myself splashing this dressing over all manner of green leaves with some crushed nuts.

SERVES 4

Salad

400g	fine green beans, stalk ends trimmed
2	heaped tablespoons coarsely chopped flat-leaf parsley
1	heaped teaspoon crushed dried rose petals

Dressing

2	teaspoons pomegranate syrup
1	teaspoon red wine vinegar
	sea salt, black pepper
4	tablespoons avocado oil

Purée

	flesh of 2 avocados
2	teaspoons lemon juice
1	tablespoon avocado oil
1	teaspoon chopped shallot
½	teaspoon sumac

Bring a large pan of salted water to the boil and cook the beans for about 3 minutes, or until just tender. Drain them into a colander, pass under the cold tap and set aside to cool.

For the dressing, whisk the pomegranate syrup and vinegar with a little seasoning in a small bowl, then whisk or stir in the oil.

Whizz all the ingredients for the avocado purée with a little seasoning in a food processor until smooth. Combine the parsley and rose petals.

To serve the salad, divide the beans between four plates. Dollop the avocado purée on top, then scatter over the parsley and rose petal mixture. Give the dressing a whisk and spoon this on top to serve.

ENERGY KCAL	CARBOHYDRATE G	SUGARS G	PROTEIN G	FAT G	SATURATED FAT G	SALT G
340	6.6	5.5	3.3	31.8	5.4	trace

Cauli Couscous Salad
with Herbs, Olives and Orange

To place this salad in perspective, that it is effectively crudités in a different guise, it gains magnitude. There are times when a few crisp vegetables dipped into a little something is just the ticket, but rarely do you find yourself wolfing them down, whereas this salad of cauliflower florets blitzed to the size of grains may have you doing just that. And, unlike a couscous salad made with wheat, it doesn't turn stodgy, which makes it ideal for lunchboxes or a welcome find in the fridge. Another take on this is pomegranate seeds and feta in lieu of tomatoes and olives.

SERVES 4

400g	cauliflower florets
1	tablespoon lemon juice
1	teaspoon finely grated orange zest
	sea salt
5	tablespoons extra virgin olive oil
2	handfuls of coarsely chopped mint
2	handfuls of coarsely chopped flat-leaf parsley
2	spring onions, trimmed and finely sliced
200g	cherry tomatoes, halved or quartered
75g	pitted green olives, halved

Trim off any excess stalk from the cauliflower florets and then whizz them in batches in a food processor until the size of couscous grains. Transfer these to a large bowl.

Whisk the lemon juice with the orange zest and some salt in a small bowl, then add the olive oil. Pour this over the cauliflower couscous and toss, then mix in all the remaining ingredients and serve.

ENERGY KCAL	CARBOHYDRATE G	SUGARS G	PROTEIN G	FAT G	SATURATED FAT G	SALT G
217	5.9	5.1	4.0	18.6	2.7	0.7

Roast Cauliflower with Coriander and Sumac

Roasting cauliflower renders the florets tender and golden at the edges, and they are especially good in the company of Middle Eastern spices. The roast onion here balances out the slight bitterness of the veg, while the sumac provides a delicate sourness.

SERVES 4

500g	cauliflower florets (each about 2–3cm)
1	red onion, peeled, halved and sliced
4	tablespoons extra virgin olive oil, plus extra for dressing
	sea salt
1	heaped teaspoon coriander seeds, coarsely ground
	sumac
2	handfuls of rocket
	squeeze of lemon juice

Preheat the oven to 190°C fan/210°C electric/gas mark 6½. Arrange the cauliflower in a single layer in a large roasting pan (e.g. 38 x 25cm), then mix in the onion, separating out the strands. Drizzle over 4 tablespoons of olive oil, season with salt and scatter over the ground coriander seeds. Roast for 30 minutes until golden at the edges, stirring halfway through. Liberally dust with sumac.

Toss the rocket with olive oil to coat the leaves, plus a squeeze of lemon and a pinch of salt. Serve the vegetables with the dressed leaves mixed in.

ENERGY KCAL	CARBOHYDRATE G	SUGARS G	PROTEIN G	FAT G	SATURATED FAT G	SALT G
137	6.7	5.6	3.6	10.1	1.5	trace

Roast Romanesco and Spring Onion Salad with Balsamic Dressing

Romanesco, with its spiralling minarets, is always a show-stopper and here it makes a lovely roast salad flavoured with nuts and capers. Hempseed oil bridges the gap between the full-on aroma of hazelnut and the more discreet presence of rapeseed. But any nutty oil will serve you well, including the less usual ones such as pine nut or pumpkin seed. You can either serve this salad warm when the veggies come out of the oven, or leave them to cool. Use cauliflower florets if you can't find a Romanesco.

SERVES 4

1	Romanesco, cut into florets (approx. 400g)
4	jumbo spring onions (or 8 standard), trimmed and cut diagonally into 2–3cm lengths
3	tablespoons hempseed or hazelnut oil
	sea salt, black pepper
150g	small cherry tomatoes, quartered
2	teaspoons balsamic vinegar
1	tablespoon small (non-pareil) capers, rinsed
2	handfuls of rocket
2	tablespoons chopped Brazil nuts
1	teaspoon lemon thyme leaves (optional)

Preheat the oven to 190°C fan/210°C electric/gas mark 6½. Arrange the Romanesco and spring onions in a large roasting pan that holds them snugly in a single layer. Drizzle over 2 tablespoons of oil, season and toss well to coat, then roast for 20–25 minutes until lightly golden, stirring halfway through.

Meanwhile, toss the tomatoes with a little salt and set aside for 15 minutes. Stir in the balsamic vinegar, the remaining oil and the capers. Transfer the roast veg to a large serving dish and mix in the rocket. Spoon over the tomato mixture and scatter over the Brazil nuts, and thyme leaves, if wished.

ENERGY KCAL	CARBOHYDRATE G	SUGARS G	PROTEIN G	FAT G	SATURATED FAT G	SALT G
201	5.1	4.3	6.8	15.6	2.4	0.2

Fricassée of Peas,
Beans and Mushrooms

This is a celebration of all the young green peas and beans we associate with late spring, and while button mushrooms are in keeping with being small and tender, some wild mushrooms would make the day. Either eat it as an aside, or add some edamame bean noodles and scatter with Parmesan as a main.

SERVES 6

50g	unsalted butter
	sea salt, black pepper
½	teaspoon caster sugar
200g	fine French beans, stalk ends trimmed, halved
200g	sugar snaps, stalk ends trimmed
200g	shelled fresh peas
1	tablespoon extra virgin olive oil, plus extra for serving
300g	button mushrooms, stalks trimmed
	large handful of coarsely chopped flat-leaf parsley

Bring 300ml of water to the boil in a medium-large saucepan with half the butter, ½ teaspoon of salt and the sugar. Add the beans and sugar snaps, bring back to the boil, cover and cook over a medium-low heat for 4 minutes, stirring in the peas after 1 minute. Drain off the liquid.

Meanwhile, fry the mushrooms. Heat the remaining butter and the olive oil in a large non-stick frying pan over a medium-high heat, and once the foam subsides, add the mushrooms. Fry for several minutes, stirring frequently, until golden, seasoning them towards the end. Fold in the vegetables and fry for a minute or so longer, then check the seasoning and fold in the parsley. Serve with extra oil drizzled over.

ENERGY KCAL	CARBOHYDRATE G	SUGARS G	PROTEIN G	FAT G	SATURATED FAT G	SALT G
101	6.2	4.0	4.9	5.4	1.1	trace

Aubergine Bruschettas

A thin slipper of caramelised aubergine can carry most bruschetta adornments. A mélange will stand as a fine first course or light summer lunch. These amounts allow for a couple of each kind of bruschetta that will do for about four people if you make up all of them. If you prefer just one type, scale up the quanitites accordingly. Although they are at their best eaten fresh, any leftovers will undoubtedly get eaten the day after.

SERVES 4

2	aubergines, sliced 1cm thick lengthways
approx. 4	tablespoons extra virgin olive oil
	sea salt, black pepper

Parma Ham

2	slices Parma ham

Tomato

100g	ripe tomatoes, diced
1	spring onion, trimmed
1	teaspoon finely chopped medium-hot green or red chilli

Mozzarella and Olive

50g	buffalo mozzarella
25g	pitted black olives
	few tiny basil leaves

Beans with Mint

40g	cooked edamame beans
1	teaspoon lemon juice, plus a pinch of finely grated zest
1	heaped teaspoon finely chopped mint
15g	finely shaved pecorino

Preheat the oven to 200°C fan/220°C electric/gas mark 7. You should have about eight aubergine slices, excluding the ends. Roast these scraps too as they make delicious snacks.

Arrange the slices on non-stick baking sheets, brush either side with oil and season the top. Roast for 15 minutes, then turn using a spatula and roast for a further 15 minutes until golden. These are good hot or cold, but best eaten on the same day. Transfer to a serving plate before assembling the toppings of your choice.

To create a simple yet delicious bruschetta, drape two aubergine slices with a slice of Parma ham each.

Place the tomatoes in a medium bowl and season with salt. Thinly slice the spring onion and add to the tomatoes with the chilli and a teaspoon of oil. Stir, then pile onto two aubergine slices.

Tear the mozzarella into 2–3cm pieces and split the olives in half. Arrange these over two aubergine slices and scatter over a few basil leaves.

For the bean topping, combine the edamame beans, lemon juice, zest and mint in a medium bowl with a teaspoon of oil. Stir to coat, then pile onto two aubergine slices. Scatter over the cheese.

Arrange your chosen bruschetta on a large platter and serve.

ENERGY KCAL	CARBOHYDRATE G	SUGARS G	PROTEIN G	FAT G	SATURATED FAT G	SALT G
272	5.5	4.2	8.5	23.0	5.5	0.9

Roast Broccoli with Feta

I am addicted to the long-stem broccoli variety, and withdrawal symptoms set in when they are unavailable, so devising a good use for a humble flowering head has been a long-time quest. It is so very dull boiled, meaning the more ways of cooking this poor cousin the better. Use nuts rather than feta for a veagn dish. Spread the florets out to give them plenty of space to colour and to ensure it is deliciously crispy, coat with plenty of oil and preheat the roasting pan.

SERVES 3

400g	head of broccoli
3	tablespoons rapeseed oil
	finely grated zest of 1 lemon
	sea salt, black pepper
75g	feta, crumbled
	chopped flat-leaf parsley (optional)

Preheat the oven to 200°C fan/220°C electric/gas mark 7 with a large roasting pan inside. Cut the broccoli florets off the stem, halving large ones downwards, into 4–5cm florets.

Toss the broccoli with the oil, lemon zest and a little seasoning in a large bowl and spread over the roasting pan. Roast for 10 minutes, then turn the pieces; the flat sides will crisp up especially well. Roast for a further 5 minutes, scatter over the feta and roast for a final 5 minutes. Serve hot or at room temperature, scooping up the toasted cheese, and scattered with parsley, if wished.

ENERGY KCAL	CARBOHYDRATE G	SUGARS G	PROTEIN G	FAT G	SATURATED FAT G	SALT G
230	3.6	3.0	9.7	18.5	4.4	0.7

Tomato and Herb Salad

There is always another spin on the simplicity of a tomato salad, a standby that goes with so many dishes, from dips to a grilled chop or chicken fillet. Leafy herbs and onion are fantastic in the company of a mix of tomatoes. Use it as a base and build it up with nuts, cheese, olives and the like.

SERVES 6

150g	cherry tomatoes
150g	tomatoes on the vine
2	beefsteak tomatoes, cored, halved if large
	sea salt
1	small red onion, peeled, halved and finely sliced
4	tablespoons extra virgin olive oil
2–3	tablespoons each chopped flat-leaf parsley, mint and basil

Cut the cherry tomatoes in half and thickly slice the other varieties. Combine all the tomatoes on a large serving plate, season with salt, then set aside for 15 minutes. (No harm will come to them if this stretches to an hour or so.)

Shortly before serving, mix in the onion and pour over the olive oil, then mix in three-quarters of the herbs, scattering the remainder over the top.

ENERGY KCAL	CARBOHYDRATE G	SUGARS G	PROTEIN G	FAT G	SATURATED FAT G	SALT G
115	5.5	5.2	1.2	8.7	1.3	trace

Coconut Cashew Gado Gado Salad

Lots of dipping going on here, and the seaweed thins act as little wraps for the other ingredients. As well as standing in for supper in its own right, this makes for easy drinks-time grazing or a communal starter.

SERVES 6

Salad

150g	green beans, stalk ends trimmed
12	cooked and peeled quail eggs*
¼	cucumber, peeled, halved lengthways and thinly sliced into long strips
½	red pepper, deseeded and cut into thin strips 5–7cm long
6	radishes, trimmed and halved downwards
150g	cooked and peeled king prawns (optional)
1–2 x 5g	finely sliced nori or crisp seaweed thins

Dressing

200g	roast salted cashews
1	tablespoon coarsely chopped medium-hot red chilli
approx. 100ml	coconut milk or water
2	tablespoons lime juice
1	tablespoon dark soy sauce (e.g. Kikkoman)
½	teaspoon palm or caster sugar
	cayenne pepper
	black and white sesame seeds

For the salad, bring a medium pan of salted water to the boil, add the green beans and cook for 3 minutes or until just tender. Drain into a colander, run under the cold tap and set aside to cool.

For the dressing, whizz the cashew nuts in a food processor to fine crumbs, then continue to whizz for 2–3 minutes until they form a stiff nut butter. With the motor still running, add the chilli and then gradually add the coconut milk or water, lime juice and soy sauce. Add the sugar and season with a generous sprinkling of cayenne pepper. The dressing should be a thick trickling consistency. Transfer to a bowl. (The recipe can be prepared to this point several hours in advance – see storage below.)

If necessary, give the dressing a stir to loosen, then scatter with sesame seeds. Place the bowl of dressing in the middle of a large serving dish, and arrange all the salad ingredients around the outside.

If you're making the dressing more than a few hours in advance, cover and chill. Gently rewarm in a bowl set over a pan with a little simmering water in it, adding a little more coconut milk or water to achieve the right consistency. It will keep well for several days. Cover and chill the beans too.

If cooking your own, bring a small pan of water to the boil, carefully lower in the quail eggs and cook for 2½–3 minutes, then drain and refill the pan with cold water and leave them to cool before peeling.

ENERGY KCAL	CARBOHYDRATE G	SUGARS G	PROTEIN G	FAT G	SATURATED FAT G	SALT G
289	9.3	5.0	16.2	19.8	4.1	1.0

Sweet Satisfaction

Without doubt the most challenging arena for the low carber revolves around dessert, as by and large the sweeter the food the more carbs it will contain. And the more carbs it contains the more likely it is to involve the addition of sugar in various forms. Even fruit comes on a sliding scale, with those that contain just modest amounts of sugar such as strawberries, blueberries, raspberries and melon, and those with really quite high levels such as bananas, grapes and cherries. To some extent you can gauge which fruits are likely to contain substantial amounts, those that have you puckering – rhubarb, gooseberries, lemons and limes – would seem unlikely to contain a great deal, but this isn't the whole story. Who would imagine that lychees would be particularly high?

So, while we need to factor in the differing amounts of carbs contained in different fruits for the remit of this book, as a food group, fruits still offer the most nutritious source of sugar. They are packaged in such a way that the sugars come well diluted in water, you have the benefit of fibre and a variety of vitamins, minerals and phytochemicals.

Beyond this natural sweetness, we really need to look to sweeteners to take care of the remainder, if we are to avoid the empty energy of concentrated sugar sources. Although natural sweeteners such as honey, maple syrup, agave and date syrup are frequently billed as being 'sugar free', this is far from the truth. In fact, honey contains more energy or calories per teaspoon than table sugar. It may be they haven't been refined and therefore tick the 'natural' box, and contain a few vitamins and minerals, but don't be fooled into thinking that these ingredients are a low-sugar alternative. They still count as added sugars.

Having researched the various alternative sweeteners that offer a way of minimizing our intake of added sugars, my own preference and is either for erythritol on its own, or blended with stevia (see pages 13–14). Stevia has a particular identity, or taste profile, that tends to hint of liquorice and slight bitterness, and the erythritol balances this out. If, however, a sweetener containing erythritol doesn't say GMO-free, then it probably isn't given the increasing amount of GMO corn being produced globally, so ideally look for an organic brand or one that clearly indicates its free-from status. It is also worth being aware that there is no standard strength of sweetness, so in the recipes that follow, the guidance is either to add the sweetener to taste, or to add the equivalent to a specified quantity of sugar. I can recommend the Sukrin brand.

Apple and Blueberry Frittata

This semi-sweet omelette has something of a clafoutis about it. In the way of sweetness there is just a little stevia, otherwise the natural sugars in the fruit and spices that we associate with baking evoke comfort.

SERVES 6

4	medium eggs
100ml	skimmed milk
1½	tablespoons granulated stevia (i.e. equivalent to 1½ tablespoons sugar)
	small pinch of saffron filaments (approx. 10), ground and blended with 1 teaspoon boiling water
1	teaspoon vanilla extract
	finely grated zest of 1 lemon, plus 1 tablespoon juice
20g	unsalted butter
1	eating apple, peeled, cored and thinly sliced lengthways
75g	blueberries
25g	ricotta or young goat's cheese
1	tablespoon dark rum
	ground cinnamon, for dusting

Whizz the eggs, milk, stevia, the saffron liquor and vanilla extract in a blender until foamy, then add the lemon zest and juice and whizz again.

Preheat the grill. Melt half the butter in a 24cm non-stick frying pan with a heatproof handle over a medium heat and fry the apple slices for a few minutes until translucent and lightly coloured, turning the slices and stirring frequently, then transfer to a bowl.

Add half the remaining butter to the pan and swirl to melt, then tip in the egg mixture and cook for 3 minutes. Just before the end of this time, scatter the apple slices over the surface, along with the blueberries, and dot with the remaining butter and ricotta or goat's cheese. Place under the grill for about 3 minutes until golden and puffy at the sides, then drizzle over the rum and dust with cinnamon. The frittata is best enjoyed after about 15 minutes of standing, or freshly cooled.

ENERGY KCAL	CARBOHYDRATE G	SUGARS G	PROTEIN G	FAT G	SATURATED FAT G	SALT G
128	6.0	5.3	7.0	7.5	3.5	0.3

Mango Ice

Such is the intensely sweet and fragrant nature of mangoes, there is no call for additional sugar here. I relish this, as someone who finds most ices either too rich or too sweet, this one is high in protein and low in fat with just the right sweetness.

SERVES 6

300g	frozen mango flesh (about 2 fruit), cut into 1cm dice*
300g	quark
2	tablespoons lemon juice
3	passionfruit, halved

Peel the frozen mango off the paper (see tip below) and place in a food processor with the quark. Whizz to a thick, sticky ice cream, scraping down the bowl as necessary to break up any clumps, adding the lemon juice towards the end. If not serving straight away, you can pop the ice into the freezer for up to an hour.

To serve, divide between six small cupped bowls and drizzle over the passionfruit seeds.

If the ice freezes solid it will set with ice crystals. But, leave it to soften at room temperature for 30–60 minutes until you can cut it into chunks, and then simply re-whizz to a thick and sticky consistency in a food processor.

Line a plastic container with baking paper, and spread the mango out in a single layer, as far as possible without touching. You can then make a second layer on top, if necessary, with more paper in between, and freeze overnight.

ENERGY KCAL	CARBOHYDRATE G	SUGARS G	PROTEIN G	FAT G	SATURATED FAT G	SALT G
79	9.6	9.5	7.9	0.2	0.1	0.1

Berry Compote with Vanilla Yogurt

This makes for a delectable weekend brunch as well as providing a sweet treat at the end of lunch or dinner. It plays to the natural sweetness of the fruit, so only add the stevia if you feel it needs it, but in season this shouldn't be necessary.

SERVES 6

200g	raspberries
4	teaspoons granulated stevia (i.e. equivalent to 4 teaspoons sugar)
2	teaspoons lemon juice
150g	blueberries
150g	strawberries, hulled and quartered
500g	quark or 0%-fat Greek yogurt
1	teaspoon vanilla bean paste
1	tablespoon single cream
2	tablespoons finely chopped pistachios

Put the raspberries, stevia (if using) and lemon juice in a blender and whizz to a purée. Pass through a sieve into a medium bowl, and fold in the blueberries and strawberries, then cover and chill for up to a couple of hours.

Beat the quark or yogurt with the vanilla bean paste and cream. This can also be prepared well in advance, in which case, cover and chill.

Just before serving, divide the vanilla yogurt between six small cocktail bowls, spoon the fruit and sauce in the centre and scatter with nuts.

ENERGY KCAL	CARBOHYDRATE G	SUGARS G	PROTEIN G	FAT G	SATURATED FAT G	SALT G
118	9.3	9.2	13.3	1.9	0.5	0.1

Papaya Creams

Here a fresh papaya purée partners a light creamy mousse. It relies on the natural sugars in the fruit, strawberry powder and vanilla. And, like other desserts in this section, it offers a calmer sweetness, one that will come as a relief to those who have eschewed sugar and find commercial products overly sweet.

SERVES 6

500g	papaya flesh (approx. 3–4 fruit)
1½	tablespoons lemon juice
2	teaspoons freeze-dried strawberry powder
250g	quark
50g	soured cream
½	teaspoon vanilla bean paste
3	small strawberries, hulled and thinly sliced downwards

Whizz the papaya, lemon juice and strawberry powder to a purée in a food processor and divide between six 150ml glasses or ramekins. Then combine the quark and soured cream with the vanilla bean paste in a medium bowl. You can prepare these several hours in advance, in which case cover and chill.

To serve, dollop the cream on top of the papaya purée and decorate with the strawberry slices.

ENERGY KCAL	CARBOHYDRATE G	SUGARS G	PROTEIN G	FAT G	SATURATED FAT G	SALT G
92	10.1	10.0	6.6	2.2	1.3	0.1

Strawberry and Pomegranate Granita

A dramatically vermilion icy slush of pomegranate and strawberries. This way of making a granita does away with all that stirring; simply make some fruit ice cubes in advance and you're seconds away.

SERVES 4

200g	chilled strawberries, hulled, plus a few slivers to decorate
400ml	pomegranate juice, frozen in cubes*
2	tablespoons pomegranate seeds

Purée the strawberries in a food processor, then press through a sieve into a bowl. Return the purée to the clean food-processing bowl, add the pomegranate ice cubes and whizz to a thick slush, stirring the mixture several times to ensure it is smooth and there are no mini icebergs in there.

Pile into four 150ml ramekins or small bowls, and scatter over a few slivers of strawberry and the pomegranate seeds, then serve.

The night beforehand, fill a couple of large ice-cube trays with the pomegranate juice and freeze.

ENERGY KCAL	CARBOHYDRATE G	SUGARS G	PROTEIN G	FAT G	SATURATED FAT G	SALT G
77	15.6	15.6	0.6	0.3	trace	0.0

Kiwi and Passionfruit Cocktail

Save this one for when you can access a heady, perfumed, orange-fleshed melon; the Charentais are the pinnacle. It's another lovely elegant cocktail that does for breakfast as well as a light everyday dessert. Drizzle over a teaspoon of honey or maple syrup if you have a particularly sweet tooth.

SERVES 2

2	kiwi fruit, skinned and cut into 1–2cm dice
100g	orange-fleshed melon (e.g. Charentais), cut into 1–2cm dice
2	passionfruit, halved
150g	medium-fat fromage frais (approx. 4% fat)
	lime wedges, to serve

Combine the kiwi fruit, melon and seeds of one of the passionfruit in a medium bowl. Divide half of this between two small bowls or glasses. Spoon the fromage frais on top, then the remaining mixed fruit, and drizzle over the remaining passionfruit seeds. (These can be made up to a couple of hours in advance, and chilled.)

Serve with lime wedges to add a little zing.

ENERGY KCAL	CARBOHYDRATE G	SUGARS G	PROTEIN G	FAT G	SATURATED FAT G	SALT G
127	16.4	16.3	6.0	2.7	1.5	0.2

Strawberry Chia Pudding

I never thought I would grow to love chia seeds, but every now and again they offer themselves up as the solution to a dilemma, such as how to create a dessert with the comfort of a traditional rice pudding, one that is not only full of goodness but ready in a jiffy – and that bag of little black seeds in the cupboard saves the day.

This plays to the comfort that we are seeking, but instead of all that cream and sugar and refined carbs, we get a few chia seeds, with some strawberries and nuts. This is a concentrated pudding, so you don't want a big bowlful, a small ramekin should suffice.

SERVES 4

200g	quark
1½	tablespoons granulated stevia (i.e. equivalent to 1½ tablespoons sugar)
	pinch of freshly grated nutmeg
	pinch of fine sea salt
½	teaspoon vanilla bean paste
2	teaspoons lemon juice
400g	strawberries, hulled and roughly chopped
50g	chia seeds

TO SERVE

50g	raspberries or blueberries
2	teaspoons soured cream
1	teaspoon finely chopped pistachio nuts

Combine the quark with the stevia, nutmeg, salt, vanilla bean paste and lemon juice in a medium bowl.

Whizz the strawberries to a purée in a blender. Pour this into a small non-stick saucepan and stir in the chia seeds. Bring to the boil and simmer over a low heat for a couple of minutes, stirring almost constantly to stop the mixture from catching on the base, then transfer to a large bowl. Whisk in the quark mixture.

Divide between four small bowls or ramekins. Serve warm with a few berries scattered in the centre, about half a teaspoon of soured cream and a pinch of nuts on top.

You can also serve the strawberry puds cold, in which case reduce the quantity of chia seeds to 30g. Cover and chill for a couple of hours, and decorate them just before serving.

ENERGY KCAL	CARBOHYDRATE G	SUGARS G	PROTEIN G	FAT G	SATURATED FAT G	SALT G
173	11.1	9.4	10.6	6.9	1.6	0.1

Raspberry Coconut Ice Cream

This has a decadently silky finish, courtesy of the coconut yogurt, and the mystery guest, avocado. Nothing in the colour of this ice gives it away, and most don't get further than 'yogurt' as a suggestion if you ask them to guess, unless they've been watching you in the kitchen out of the corner of their eye. And you can experiment with other fruits – strawberries, blueberries, mango, peaches... anything soft, sweet and jammy.

SERVES 6

2	small avocados, halved and stoned
150g	coconut yogurt
2	teaspoons lime juice
2	heaped tablespoons granulated stevia (i.e. equivalent to 2 heaped tablespoons sugar)
200g	frozen raspberries*
3	passionfruit, halved
6	strawberries, hulled and quartered

Scoop the avocado flesh into the bowl of a food processor, add the yogurt, lime juice and stevia and whizz until smooth. Add the frozen raspberries and continue to whizz to a thick, sticky ice cream, scraping down the bowl as necessary to break up any clumps. If not serving straight away, you can pop the ice into the freezer for up to an hour.

To serve, divide between six small cupped bowls, drizzle over the passionfruit seeds and scatter over the strawberries.

If the ice freezes solid it will set with ice crystals. But you can leave it to soften at room temperature for 30–60 minutes until you can cut it into chunks, and then simply re-whizz to a thick and sticky consistency in a food processor.

*Ideally freeze your own raspberries, to ensure they remain separate. If you have bought the raspberries in a plastic tub, you can achieve this by lining the base of the tub with baking paper and spreading over a single layer without touching. You can then make a second layer on top, with more paper in between, and freeze overnight.

ENERGY KCAL	CARBOHYDRATE G	SUGARS G	PROTEIN G	FAT G	SATURATED FAT G	SALT G
179	5.4	4.0	2.3	14.7	7.0	trace

Blackberry and Blueberry Cocktail

I love the rich colours of this ensemble, and the textures too. This takes care of your fruit for the day, a small powerhouse of nutrients. It is staggeringly pretty, and it could certainly raise its game to mark the end of a lovely dinner – just dress it up with a teaspoon of crème fraîche or raw cream, or a creamy Greek yogurt.

SERVES 2

200g	blackberries
2	tablespoons orange juice
2	basil leaves, plus a few tiny leaves to serve
1	heaped teaspoon granulated stevia (i.e. equivalent to 1 heaped teaspoon sugar)
40g	blueberries
30g	pomegranate seeds
1	teaspoon toasted and chopped or halved hazelnuts

Purée the blackberries with the orange juice, basil leaves and stevia in a blender, then pass this through a sieve into a medium bowl. Spread the purée over the base of two small shallow bowls. Scatter the blueberries and pomegranate seeds in a line across the centre, and then the hazelnuts and a few tiny basil leaves. Cover and chill for up to half a day.

ENERGY KCAL	CARBOHYDRATE G	SUGARS G	PROTEIN G	FAT G	SATURATED FAT G	SALT G
88	10.8	10.2	1.7	1.8	0.1	trace

Chocolate, Date and Orange Mousse

This chocolate mousse offers a note of restraint within its genre. The flavour of the cocoa, the orange and hazelnuts all find a voice, with the sweetness bolstered by dates and orange.

SERVES 6

4	Medjool dates (approx. 80g), pitted and coarsely chopped
3	tablespoons smooth orange juice
100g	dark chocolate (approx. 85% cocoa), broken into pieces
4	medium eggs, separated
1	teaspoon finely grated orange zest
1	tablespoon roasted and chopped hazelnuts

Put the dates and orange juice in a small saucepan, bring to the boil and simmer for 1 minute, mashing the dates into the liquid until you have a thick paste. Transfer the mixture to a food processor.

Gently melt the chocolate in a large heatproof bowl set over a pan with a little simmering water in it. This needs to be at room temperature, so leave it to cool a little.

Add the egg yolks to the dates in the food processor and whizz to a purée, then trickle in the melted chocolate and whizz to mix. Scrape the chocolate mixture, which will be thick and sticky, into a large bowl.

Whisk the egg whites to fluffy peaks in another large bowl using an electric whisk. Add half of these to the chocolate base and beat until smooth using a wooden spoon. Fold in the remaining egg whites in two goes, and divide between six 100ml little cups or ramekins. Scatter over a little orange zest and some chopped hazelnuts. Place the ramekins on a plate or in a baking dish, and pop into the freezer for 20 minutes. They will be soft and moussey when they come out of the freezer, ready to eat, if wished. (They will set further with chilling in the fridge, and can be stored for up to a couple of days, loosely covered with clingfilm.)

ENERGY KCAL	CARBOHYDRATE G	SUGARS G	PROTEIN G	FAT G	SATURATED FAT G	SALT G
210	14.1	11.2	6.8	13.3	6.3	0.2

INDEX

Acknowledgements

My thanks to the wonderful team at Kyle Books for all the work that has gone into producing this beautiful book. To Kyle Cathie and Judith Hannam for giving me the opportunity, to Hannah Coughlin for your meticulous editing and project management, and to Julia Barder and Victoria Scales for doing so much to take the project forward, and to Nic Jones and Gemma John for steering the production. And to Stephanie Evans for copy-editing the manuscript.

To Con Poulos and Susie Theodorou and your assistants for your endless creativity and fabulous pictures, I will always be in awe of the way you work your magic. To Marie-Helene Jeeves for the charming illustrations that have added so much fun to the book. It has been a treat to have David Eldridge and his team at Two Associates designing the book, bringing together the many different threads.

My journey exploring the science behind Low Carb diets began with Dr Alexander Miras, Senior Clinical Lecturer in Endocrinology at Imperial College, thank you for inspiring me to take that road, and to Alexandra King and all the exceptional tutors within the Nutrition Department at St Mary's University, your knowledge, experience and support have been invaluable.

To my agent Lizzy Kremer at David Higham, your calm wisdom is the foundation for what follows. To Angela Mason, Associate Editor of YOU Magazine in the Mail on Sunday, with whom so many ideas first take root. And to those closest to me, Jonnie, Rothko and Louis, for your love and support and endless encouragement, you make cooking the pleasure that it is.

References

Accurso, A., Bernstein, R.K., Dahlqvist, A., Draznin, B., Feinman, R.D., Fine, E.J., Gleed, A., Jacobs, D.B., Larson, G., Lustig, R.H., Manninen, A.H., McFarlane, S.I., Morrison, K., Nielsen, J.V., Ravnskov, U., Roth, K.S., Silvestre, R., Sowers, J.R., Sundberg, R., Volek, J.S., Westman, E.C., Wood, R.J., Wortman, J., and Vernon, M.C. (2008). Dietary carbohydrate restriction in type 2 diabetes mellitus and metabolic syndrome: time for a critical appraisal. Nutrition and Metabolism, 5(1), 9-9.